I N V E S T I G A Ç Ã O

I

IMPRENSA DA UNIVERSIDADE DE COIMBRA
COIMBRA UNIVERSITY PRESS

U

EDITION
Imprensa da Universidade de Coimbra
Email: imprensa@uc.pt
URL: http//www.uc.pt/imprensa_uc
Vendas online: http://livrariadaimprensa.uc.pt

EDITORIAL COORDINATION
Imprensa da Universidade de Coimbra

GRAPHIC CONCEPTION
António Barros

IMAGE ON THE COVER
By Maria Objetiva [CC-BY-SA-2.0
(http://creativecommons.org/licenses/by-sa/2.0)],
via Wikimedia Commons

INFOGRAPHICS
Mickael Silva

PRINT BY
CreateSpace

ISBN
978-989-26-0916-4

DIGITAL ISBN
978-989-26-0917-1

DOI
http://dx.doi.org/10.14195/978-989-26-0917-1

DEMOCRACY AT WORK:
PRESSURE AND PROPAGANDA IN PORTUGAL AND BRAZIL

IMPRENSA DA
UNIVERSIDADE
DE COIMBRA
COIMBRA
UNIVERSITY
PRESS

RITA FIGUEIRAS
PAULA ESPÍRITO SANTO
ISABEL FERIN CUNHA

CONTENTS

NOTES ON CONTRIBUTORS

Helcimara de Souza Telles is professor of the Political Science Department of the Federal University of Minas Gerais (UFMG), Brazil. She is coordinator of the Research Group "Public Opinion: Political Marketing and Electoral Behaviour", in the Federal University of Minas Gerais and "Political Communication and Electoral behaviour" linked to the Latin American Association of Political Science (ALACIP). Professor Telles has published various articles in Public Opinion and Electoral Behaviour field, and organized the books *Political Communication and Electoral Behaviour in Latin America* (Telles and Moreno, UFMG, 2012); *How the elector chooses his mayor: vote and campaign in municipal elections* (Lavareda and Telles, FGV, 2011) and *From the streets to the ballot boxes: parties and elections in contemporaneous Brazil* (Telles and Lucas, EDUCS, 2004).

Isabel Ferin Cunha is an associate professor, with aggregation, of the University of Coimbra, Portugal. She is a researcher at the Center for Media and Journalism Research in the fields of analysis of media (print and television) and political communication. In 2008 she coordinated the research "Acts of Journalism and Democracy" (Paulus, 2007), the research "Telenovelas: from production to reception" (Livros Horizonte, 2011), in 2012 "Analysis of the Media" (Universidade de Coimbra, 2012), "Immigration in Portugal: an approach to Lusophone Media system" (2012).

Nuno Coimbra Mesquita is a research fellow in The Center for Public Policy Research of the University of São Paulo, Brazil. He was a post-doctoral fellow in the Department of Political Science of the University of Sao Paulo - where he was also a teaching assistant - with support from the São Paulo Research Foundation. He is member of the board of the Political Communication Research Committee of The International Political Science Association (RC22 – IPSA). Dr Mesquita's expertise is on media and democracy, and in particular how different media affect citizens' orientations toward politics.

Paula do Espírito Santo is Assistant Professor with Aggregation at the School of Social and Political Sciences (ISCSP) - University of Lisbon (UL), at the Institute of Police Sciences and Internal Security (ISCPSI), in Portugal, and is Visiting Professor at several Universities abroad. Paula Espírito Santo is Researcher at the CAPP (Centre for Public Administration and Public Policies), having produced research in the areas of political communication, social sciences methodology and political sociology, including the study of political culture and party members.

Rita Figueiras, is a professor at the Human Sciences Faculty at the Catholic University of Portugal, coordinator of the PhD program in Communication Studies at the UCP and member of the board of the Research Centre for Communication and Culture (CECC). Her work focuses on political communication, political economy of the media and journalism, particularly in the areas of public opinion, pundits, electoral campaigns, and, more broadly, the relationship between the media and democracy. Along with journal articles and book chapters, she has published several books.

INTRODUCTION

The book *Democracy at Work: Pressure and Propaganda in Portugal and Brazil* aims to address democracy both as an institutional value system and as a practice. Diversity and pluralism of voices, themes and perspectives are considered to be the elements that embody democracy as a value: a cultural understanding that revolves around people as the prime movers of democratic politics. Practice, is understood as being a type of routine behavior expressed in everyday life, meaning that action and representation are privileged sites for analyzing democracy at work from different protagonists' perspectives, who are recognized as agents of pressure and propaganda.

The different perspectives of the protagonists will be analyzed within distinct socioeconomic contexts, such as Portugal and Brazil. In addition to representing a relevant contribution to the Lusophone communication studies, and political communication studies in particular, both these countries embody a different example of the democratic process. While Western democracies have been experiencing extreme hardships, deep economic recessions and measures of political austerity following the economic crisis of 2008, countries outside the West, such as Brazil and the other BRIC, possess large economies, are thriving and their importance in the international arena is growing, but is facing an internal political turmoil. It is the aim, through the chapters on the two countries in the book, to contribute to an understanding of how democracy works when hope (on behalf of the people) and strength (on behalf of Governments) are weakening and also how those two factors impact upon politics.

In the aftermath of the 2008 global economic crisis, Western democracies have been experiencing a deep economic recession with high levels of unemployment, the loss of public subsides and jobs, and rising prices. In turn, within the context of Brazil's thriving economy several studies have revealed that the majority of that country's population is actively interested in politics and is strongly embedded in the traditional mechanisms of participation and representation, despite also being involved in other, unconventional ways. The predominance of the former should not be interpreted as a sign of either conservatism or a favorable posture towards hierarchical political relationships, as the 2013 demonstrations have showed. Instead, the combination of both of those political practices shows that Brazilians know how to take advantage of classic democratic institutions. It also demonstrates that they are able to resort to more independent forms of manifestation outside the conventional means, which may be seen as beneficial to the democratic process. At least for now, autonomous and independent ways of challenging and making demands from the Government are put into practice without questioning the institutional mechanisms of representation. Consequently, this mixed posture seems to be helping to consolidate Brazil's maturing democracy.

The book offers, therefore, complementary perspectives regarding the numerous tensions, doubts, anxieties, and complexities that are framing democracies in the 21st century. This framework revolves around the idea of the media as agents of political pressure through the news media's symbolic power as a watchdog and its ability to continually frame and reframe public debate. How are the media exerting their mediation role? And how are the media re-presenting the political world to society? Are different media voices offering diversified and complementary perspectives on politics? These questions are addressed in theoretical and empirical chapters based upon news and commentary illustrated with case studies from Brazil and Portugal.

Nuno Coimbra Mesquita in Chapter 1, 'The Different Impacts of the Media on Regime Support in Brazil', explores the way in which the media represent and mediate over a democratic regime. This empirical study evaluates how the media is relevant for understanding how Brazilian people orient themselves toward the political system. The author argues that the role of the media in political support is a complex one, and that it is not accurate to blame an anti-political bias on the part of the media for negative attitudes that citizens have regarding democracy. Even if a more critical attitude toward politics by the news media is taken as a given, there is controversy about this representing, by extension, an anti-institutional attitude.

In Chapter 2, 'Democracy, Corruption and News Coverage in Portugal', Isabel Ferin discusses such concepts theoretically, focusing on Western democracies, but giving special relevance to the Portuguese case. Principles of representative democracy, but also the emergence of new social movements craving greater democratic participation in the public sphere, are also debated. The author also addresses the procedures for disclosing corruption phenomena and their legal implications, as well as the principles of transparency of information and their consequences upon democracy.

Like the news media, comments from pundits also play a relevant role in shaping public debate. Considering the ripple effect of the pundits' agenda when analyzing public issues, Rita Figueiras argues in Chapter 3, 'Public Opinion and Punditry in Portugal' that the kind of mediation happening in such columns promotes exclusionary feelings in readers, thereby contradicting ideals of inclusion that culturally define the public sphere.

How is propaganda perceived within different democratic and economic contexts? Is political mistrust shaping the strategy of propaganda? And is this feeling of discontent effecting people's involvement in conventional politics? This second section offers insights into these matters by addressing conventional political participation, i.e. political campaigning strategies and voters' involvement in elections in the two different cultural contexts: Portugal and Brazil.

Chapter 4, 'Better or more involved in politics? The involvement of Portuguese voters in Parliamentary elections', analyses the behavior of voters in Portugal. Paula do Espírito Santo argues that the Portuguese electorate is politically participative and electorally receptive, whether it be in terms of paying attention to information about the electoral process or in terms of reflecting upon electoral issues.

In Chapter 5, 'Trust in Lula da Silva and the Brazilian presidential campaigns,'Helcimara de Souza Telles demonstrates that campaigns are relevant to the decision on how votes are cast, because they are able to articulate supply and demand in a market-regulated election, and that the Brazilian presidential campaigns of 2010 centered on the dispute over the symbolic representation of what could be called Lula's third term.

The book addresses, therefore, a set of problems and questions which are in need of urgent discussion, as their impact and consequences are deeply transforming politics and the way politics is communicated, lived and understood by its main actors in the political system, headed by the people themselves. Within this framework, Political Communication Studies has a major role in identifying and urging new diagnosis of, and insights into, the political system, its functions and structures and, above all, how both the people and political institutions can both survive crisis and improve democracy in the Lusophone world. This book aims at making an important contribution to that acknowledgment.

CHAPTER 1

MEDIA AND THE QUALITY OF DEMOCRACY: THE DIFFERENT IMPACTS OF THE MEDIA ON REGIME SUPPORT IN BRAZIL[1]

Nuno Coimbra Mesquita

Introduction

With Brazilian democracy having already surpassed the milestone of its 20 years - considering its new democratic constitution and the first direct presidential elections after military rule - support for the regime reaches its highest rates. In 1989 only 44% of Brazilians believed democracy as the best form of government. In 2006 that number reached 71% (Moisés 2008). Political support is fundamental to the understanding of the quality of democracy. After democracy spread to most countries of the world, scholarly attention has turned more to this aspect than to the analysis of the transitions themselves (Diamond and Morlino 2004).

Some of the perspectives concerning media impact on democracy point to a growing cynicism of the press in dealing with public issues, leading to the belittlement of politics and politicians in general (Patterson 1998,

[1] This chapter is a result of a post-doctoral research financed by the Fundação de Amparo à Pesquisa do Estado de São Paulo (Fapesp). An earlier version of this text was published as "Mídia e Apoio Político à Democracia no Brasil" in Moisés, J.A.; Meneguello, R. (orgs) "A Desconfiança Política e os seus Impactos na Qualidade da Democracia". São Paulo, Edusp, 2013. This text was reviewed and updated.

DOI: http://dx.doi.org/10.14195/978-989-26-0917-1_1

Cappella and Jamieson 1997). On the other hand, studies based on surveys indicate that news media exposure is associated with more democratic attitudes and trust in the regime (Norris 2000, Newton 1999). Regardless of the perspective adopted on the subject, the information about institutions in the media is an element available to citizens to form their opinions, beyond the concrete experiences they may have. Therefore, what can be said about the role played by the media in the quality of democracy? More specifically, how is public support for the democratic regime affected by media exposure?

We argue that there are two sets of multidimensionality of the phenomenon. On the one hand, public support for democracy comprises different dimensions. People can be deferential to democracy per se, but distrust their institutions; adhere to the political community, but be dissatisfied with the functioning of democracy as it presents itself, or even evaluate critically its institutions. On the other hand, media also presents itself as multidimensional. The information contained - and audience reach - are not the same in a quality newspaper or in a newscast. Television broadcasts entertainment programs with different characteristics, each with the potential to affect differently the understanding that individuals have about the affairs of the State.

The purpose of this paper is to analyze the interrelationships between these different dimensions. The main objective of this study is to evaluate how different mass media are relevant for citizens' orientations toward the political system. Is this exposure beneficial or detrimental to a democratic political culture? We argue that the media present a plural role in democratic attitudes, depending both on the specific media and on the dimension of political support taken into account. This paper focuses its analysis on five media variables: exposure to news on *newspapers, TV, radio* and *Internet*, and total *TV exposure*. We want to know if these media variables are associated positively or negatively with political support. The chosen methodological approach to the problem was statistical analyses of national public opinion surveys. Using regression models for prediction purposes, it is possible to evaluate what set of variables (media exposure) affect dependent variables (citizens' attitudes toward the political system). We use data from the survey 'Citizens' Distrust in Democratic Institutions' (2006), and from the 'Latin American Public Opinion Project' (2008).

14

The paper initially discusses the issue of political support as an aspect of the quality of the regime, reviewing the literature on the debate about the effects of mass media on the democratic process. Next, from the singularities of the Brazilian case, we present the hypotheses that orient the research. Then, we show the results of Brazilians' main media source (TV), followed by secondary news sources (newspapers, radio and the Internet). The final considerations try to reflect on the role played by the media in the quality of democracy.

Media and the Quality of Democracy

Attitudes of democratic support are essential for the quality of the regime. Studies on democratic quality intensified after the Third Wave of democratization, and also after signs of growing discontent with actual regime performance of older democracies. Therefore, a greater academic effort was made to investigate *how* regimes really work, instead of questions of *why* the transitions occurred. Diamond and Morlino (2004) defined the rule of law, competition, participation, accountability, freedom, equality and responsiveness as crucial dimensions for democratic quality. These authors suggest that the quality of the regime varies as much as these dimensions interact between themselves.

We turn our attention here to the responsiveness dimension. Since it has to do with consonance between policies adopted by elected officials and aspirations of electors-citizens, it is related to the level of satisfaction with regime performance and the legitimacy that participants of the polity ascribe to it. Hence, under this perspective, the study of political support is crucial to the understanding of the quality of democracy. The question of political support comprehends different dimensions. Easton's (1965) original idea of diffuse support – i.e. attitudes toward the system as a whole – and specific support – i.e. concerning citizens' satisfaction with government and political leadership performances – has been further elaborated in some theoretical approaches.

Some authors have identified five levels of this type of attitude: support for the *political community* (related to bonds between citizens and the nation-state, usually measured by feelings of national pride); for the *democratic regime per se* (related to democratic adherence as an ideal, connected with values such as freedom, rule of law, participation and tolerance); for the actual performance of the democratic system, measured by *satisfaction with the regime*; for democratic institutions (measured by levels of *trust* in them) and for political leaders (related to the *evaluation* of politicians and political leaders) (Norris 1999, Moisés and Carneiro 2010).

Associated with the question of adherence to regime principles is the intermediary function of political parties. Understood as a requirement for the democratic ideal, their valorization constitutes one of the essential elements of this adherence. This valorization can be seen as composed both by normative and pragmatic orientations. The former refers to the axiological role that political parties should fulfill in democracy. Differently, the latter is the perception of the real performance of parties as well as proximity between citizens and them.

Political support, taking into account these different dimensions, has varied in consolidated democracies. While support for the community and democratic principles remained high, trust in politicians and evaluation of the performance of the democratic system have fallen in many consolidated as well as young democracies (Norris 1999, Dalton 1999). In Brazil, public support for the regime presents a paradoxical picture. While adherence to democracy as an ideal reaches 2/3 of citizens - having increased since 1989, when it reached only about half of them - trust in institutions, evaluation of the main actors and satisfaction with the democratic system have inverse levels (Moisés 2007).

Different theoretical perspectives try to explain what determines these attitudes toward the political system. Studies of political culture, for example, emphasize aspects like political values or normative orientations of citizens. In this sense, this variety of shared attitudes and beliefs - like political interest, tolerance, national pride, political efficacy, and institutional and interpersonal trust – are supposed to influence the conceptions that inform people's involvement with public life. Although this theory postulates that these orientations are long lasting, changes are expected to occur. That is the case of processes of economic and social modernization, for example (Inglehart and Welzel 2005). Therefore, aspects such as political orientations and values are seen as influencing citizens' choice to accept the democratic regime as their preferable alternative (Almond and Verba 1963, Inglehart 2002).

Institutional theories of democracy, nevertheless, not considering these factors, believe in the actual performance of governments and its institutions as elements that explain phenomena like trust or regime support (Coleman 1990, North 1990). These perspectives should not necessarily mean rival hypotheses. Political culture, as well as institutional evaluation, can affect in different ways individuals' experiences and influence their political orientations (Moisés 2010).

The importance of the media to explain adherence, likewise, should not be seen as a challenging hypothesis. Given the importance of the media in contemporary societies, in their role of informing citizens over public issues, we argue that they influence public perception of institutions and democracy. From this point of view, the influence of the media should not be seen dissociated from the culturalist or institutionalist approaches. The reason is that, on the one hand, they are responsible for disseminating practical information about institutions. This information, together with actual experience that citizens have with them, provides a base for individuals to form their attitudes regarding the system. On the other hand, the media are also responsible for transmitting values, which could influence more normative perceptions that citizens have of their political system. The complex relationship between politics and communicative processes has been studied under a convergence of different disciplines and ascribed the general label of political communication. Among diverse research interests in this field, different approaches try to estimate the impact of the media on citizens' values and cognition. While media malaise theories point to an adverse effect caused by an emphasis on negative aspects of political life portrayed by the media, political mobilization approach stresses that news exposure has the capacity to better inform the public, leading to a positive impact on the political process.

During the 1990's, media criticisms became common, reflecting a climate of '(...) angst about the vitality of democracy at a time of widespread cynicism about political leaders and government institutions (...)' (Norris 2000: 6). Patterson (1998) states that political parties and representative institutions have weakened in the post-industrial era. The media are increasingly expected to compensate for the defects of political institutions. They are not required just to inform citizens about current affairs or to watch for wrongdoings. It is also expected that they take a preeminent position in setting the public agenda, organizing public discussions and instructing citizens on relevant values in policy problems and issues. The media, however, are not suited for organizing public opinion and debate because of the restricted amount of time they have. Patterson (2000) also states that American journalism depicts politics as a game – in which politicians, as individuals, struggle for power – instead of as an issue. Furthermore, there is American media's adversarial stance, with a greater proportion of negative in relation to positive news. The consequence would be the disenchantment of citizens with their leaders and political institutions.

Television is also blamed for civic disengagement in contemporary society, as is the case of the disappearance of 'social capital' (Putnam 1995). Interpersonal trust - a central variable in studies of social capital - is associated with trust in democratic institutions (Moisés 2007, Rennó 2001). Thus, television has the potential to undermine, even if indirectly, trust that citizens place in public institutions.

Capella and Jamieson (1997) argue that the structure of political news has direct effects on public cynicism regarding politics, the government, political debates and campaigns. This happens as a result of the predominance in the media of what they call strategy coverage, which emphasizes the winning and loosing, the language of war, games and competition; the emphasis on the performance in opinion polls and candidate styles, and the great influence of opinion polls in the evaluation of candidates. This type of journalistic coverage would promote sensationalism and the simplification of complex issues, creating a 'spiral of cynism' in the public, fomenting disengagement both from the political process and from the press.

However, this negative view about the effects of mass media on the democratic processes is not unanimous. There is a theoretical perspective that argues that a combination of higher educational levels and increased access to political information have helped to mobilize citizens, both in terms of behavior and increasing knowledge. It is not that the media have only positive effects. Watching television may even be associated with less knowledge and understanding of politics. Nevertheless, reading newspapers and watching television news have an inverse relationship, fostering trust in institutions and satisfaction with the functioning of democracy (Newton, 1999). News media represent a 'virtuous circle' where attention to news gradually strengthens civic engagement, while civic engagement encourages the consumption of information. Attention to news media would not only be positive for trust but also for support for democratic principles (Norris 2000).

Although both perspectives converge on the concern about the harmful effects of total television exposure, it's not possible to say that the *content* watched has negative effects. As television programming is plural, each message has different meanings in terms of positive or negative stimuli for democratic quality. Studies on the impact of different programming have shown how the results are not unidirectional. Variables such as interpersonal trust and civic engagement, for example, may be fostered or undermined by TV viewership depending on the type of programming (Shah 1998, Uslaner 1998).

In Brazil, there is a gap in studies on the relationship between media and public support for democracy. There is a greater interest in the effects of the media on electoral processes (Straubhaar, Olsen and Nunes 1993, Porto 1996, Miguel 1999, 2003 and 2004). There is also an interest in content analyses, which have a common and unanimous interpretation of an antipolitical bias in Brazilian media. Journalistic coverage of politics – especially of the legislative power – is frequently characterized as being negative, focusing on themes like corruption. Even if necessary in a democracy, this investigative journalism and its antipolitical stance would have the potential to disseminate distrust and aversion to politics, creating serious obstacles to the legitimacy of the democratic regime (Chaia and Azevedo 2008, Porto 2000a, Chaia and Teixeira 2001). Notwithstanding, there is also the standpoint that this antipolitical bias, although negative in relation to politicians as individuals, does not question the system per se, having an acquiescent character in regards to the political system and its main institutions (Miguel and Coutinho 2007).

Although these studies might suggest interesting hypotheses, we understand that the media cannot be studied solely on the basis of content analysis, since the public does not interpret messages homogeneously. Individuals are capable of critically interpreting what they consume in the media. The relevance that they have, as well as other sources of information, is given in a wider context, where other interpersonal sources – such as friends, family and organizations like the church and unions – play an equally important part (Straubhaar, Olsen and Nunes 1993).

Therefore, even if the antipolitical stance of Brazilian media is taken as a given, it is questionable that they represent an obstacle to democracy, through the depiction of corruption cases that could lead to distrust in politicians and institutions as a whole. First, we need to further analyze the content of the media itself. There is a certain consensus over the fact that the media's negative attitude is restricted to a critical appraisal of public officials. The media is not accused of being cynical of the system or of its institutions. The claim is that this negative individual characterization represents, by extension, also a negative view of the system (Porto 2000a, Chaia and Azevedo 2008). In a different perspective, it could also be argued that the emphasis on conflict and negative news coverage is a democratic function of the media, which should also act as a *watchdog*, holding governments accountable for their actions (Schmitt-Beck and Voltmer 2007). Far from disturbing trust in institutions, for instance, it would be the perception that the media watch power, one of the guaranties of the general climate of trust.

Contrary to what these content analyses suggest, studies based on survey statistical analysis point to more modest and positive effects of the media on perceptions of the political system. Meneguello (2010) found a modest association between information consumption in the media – especially broadcast – and critical evaluations of the functioning of democracy and institutional distrust. On the other hand, despite a period of very negative news concerning corruption scandals, viewership of Brazil's main Newscast, *Jornal Nacional*, appeared positively associated with trust and evaluation of institutions, and with satisfaction with Brazilian democracy (Mesquita 2010). Even if we consider the uncertainty about the direction of causality, these results defy the assumption that an antipolitical stance of the media can undermine confidence that citizens have in their institutions.

Differently from what part of Brazilian literature on the subject states, therefore, citizens seem to differentiate individual misconducts from failures in the working of the institutions. Publicizing irregularities and, at the same time, the institutions responsible for investigating them, confront citizens with control and accountability mechanisms present in the democratic system. The public has, thus, conditions to evaluate positively these regime instruments. News media, furthermore, are associated with other measures of democratic quality, such as political participation (Rennó 2003), and adherence to political parties as an essential element of democracy (Schlegel 2006).

Although news media seem to play a positive role in democratic quality, entertainment programming plays a more plural one, depending on their characteristics (Shah 1998). As programming is very diverse, each with different content and implications, its study presents a challenge. In Brazil, there is the perspective that fiction (especially soap operas), present politics in a negative way. The alternative of a moral solution from outside the political field, usually by some vigilante, is often presented, which could foster authoritarian movements (Porto 2000b).

In Brazil, broadcast media use is widespread, while there are both low educational levels and significant illiteracy rates. Brazilian TV and its newscasts are a privileged source of political information. Although less Brazilians use the radio, this medium still survives as a 'niche' for obtaining news. Of those who use it for this purpose, 71,5% are from Brazilian smaller countryside cities and 62% are older than 35 years old (Meneguello 2010).

Newspapers, for their part, are characterized by low readership, cumulativeness and overlapping. Of those who read newspapers at least once a week, 83% also state they watch *Jornal Nacional* at least once a week, while the opposite is not true. Only 45% of those who state watching JN at least once a week, read newspapers the same frequency (Meneguello 2010). Despite its low circulation, the press performs an active role in denouncing corruption scandals and in setting the agenda for other media, like TV, in addition to being a 'niche' for more instructed citizens and opinion formers.

With the objective of investigating the role of the media in aspects of democratic quality, we examine here the five dimensions of political support: *democratic adherence per se, support for political community, trust* and *evaluation* of political institutions, and *satisfaction with democracy*. We add a sixth dimension to the analysis, which we consider also as an important part of democratic culture: the valorization of the *representation function of political parties*. These are the dependent variables of our study. The independent variables are: news consumption on *TV* (measured by viewership of Brazil's main newscast, *Jornal Nacional*), *newspapers*, *radio* and *Internet*, and total *TV exposure*. Through statistical analyses of two national surveys ('Citizens Distrust in Democratic Institutions', 2006 and 'Latin American Public Opinion Project', 2008), the study aims to assess the impact of exposure to the media in question on Brazilians' support for their political system.

Both mobilization and media malaise theories interpret total TV exposure as having negative effects on the public. In Brazil, there is an understanding - yet to be tested empirically - that television, by presenting an anti-political bias, could restrict interpretations available for people to understand political content (Porto 2005). Thus, it is expected that in Brazil:

H_1: Watching TV has a negative relationship with political support variables.[2]

---

[2] In the 2006 survey, it is only possible to test the variable representing the total number of hours that individuals are exposed to television. However, except for the newscast in question, it is not possible to know what other programs are being viewed. Thus, it is only possible to test the hypothesis that the total number of hours spent in front of the tv would somehow be damaging to social interactions of individuals, which, by extension, could also adversely affect variables of political support.

Mobilization theories argue that exposure to news, increasing information citizens have, foster greater support for the regime and its institutions. Political support variables comprehend two general orientations. While support for the political community, adherence to democratic values and valorization of political parties are part of more axiological and normative orientations; trust and evaluation of institutions, and satisfaction with democracy, represent a more pragmatic character. Therefore:

H_2: watching news on TV and listening to news on the radio increase political knowledge and fosters both pragmatic and axiological attitudes toward democracy.

On the other hand, newspapers and the Internet reach a more elitist public in Brazil. The low circulation of newspapers in Brazil also means a larger audience segmentation, which has a higher accumulation of information obtained from other means. Thus, this 'niche' may represent the 'critical citizen' of Norris (1999). That is, the more informed citizens who are more demanding and more critical of the performance of the regime. In this sense:

H_3: Although reading newspapers and consuming news on the Internet are positively associated with axiological orientations (support for the community, adherence to democratic values and valorization of political parties), they have a negative relationship with more pragmatic dimensions (trust and evaluation of institutions, and satisfaction with democracy).

Since our independent media variables aren't all included in one single survey, we used two surveys. For total TV exposure and JN viewership, we used 'Citizens' Distrust in Democratic Institutions' (2006).[3] For the rest of media variables the 'Latin American Public Opinion Project' (2008) survey was used.[4] Although the language of causality is used in this text, at times, it is implicit that what we talk about is correlations, since it is not possible to attribute cause and effect relationships with this type of data.

---

[3] Coordinated by professors Dr. José Álvaro Moisés (usp) and Dr. Rachel Meneguello (unicamp).

[4] Statistical treatment and interpretation of the data, however, are my own. Both surveys used national probability sample design of voting-age adults. "Citizens' Distrust Survey (2006)": 2004 interviews. Lapop survey (2008): 1,497 interviews. The sample was stratified by regions (north, northeastern, mid-west, southeastern and south) and by urban and rural areas. www.lapopsurveys.org.

TV and political support: television and newscast exposure

The first results, obtained with the 2006 'Citizens Distrust in Democratic Institutions' survey show how Brazilians' main media source affects political support. Since dependent variables are ordinal, we opted for performing a categorical regression procedure.[5] In all models we included socioeconomic variables as control variables. While total TV exposure was expected to have negative associations with political support, Brazil's main evening news, *Jornal Nacional* (hereafter referred to as JN), was expected to display associations in the opposite direction, i.e., fostering positive attitudes regarding democracy and its institutions.

In general, and as our hypothesis stated, TV viewership is negatively correlated with political support, although in a less clear cut way than expected. The dimension of democratic adherence, as well as evaluation of institutions, points to this direction as Table 1 depicts. Those who most watch TV agree more with 'governments disrespecting laws in times of trouble', that the President should 'disregard Congress and parties in times of trouble', that they 'would give a blank check to a savior leader that solved problems of the country' and that 'only a dictatorship can 'fix' Brazil'. TV viewership is also associated with a more critical appraisal of institutions (Federal Government, political parties, congressmen and senators). The dimension of satisfaction with democracy is not associated with this media variable.

However, both trust in institutions and valorization of political parties have more ambiguous results. The data presented in Table 1 reveal that, although television is associated with the idea of a single party system, it makes individuals closer to parties. As for trust in institutions, while

---

[5] (*Optimal Scalling* in SPSS). Categorical Regression quantifies categorical data ascribing numerical values to categories. This results in a linear optimal linear equation for the transformed variables. All variables in the study were recoded for a positive coefficient (Beta) to always represent greater support for democracy. Therefore, for dependent variables such as "prefers democracy than savior leader", a positive Beta would represent greater **agreement** with the phrase. For phrases like "only a dictatorship can fix Brazil", a positive coefficient represents greater **disagreement**. Therefore, all positive coefficients of the study refer to a positive impact for the dimension in question. See Methodological Appendix for formulation of variables.

this media variable is associated with less trust in the judiciary, the police and entrepreneurs, it fosters a better assessment of the Armed Forces, the Federal Government, the fire department, political parties and the President. As for the dimension of support for the political community, the relationship goes in the opposite direction as expected, fostering more pride in nationality.

These results confirm the negative association between exposure to television and various aspects of the quality of democracy (Putnam 1995, Newton 1999, Shah 1998). However, as in the 'Citizens Distrust' survey there are no variables with specific contents watched, it can only be argued that *how much* TV individuals watch seems to be detrimental to perceptions of democracy. As for *what* is watched, further studies would be needed to support or reject theories about what specific contents may represent.

Table 1: TV, Newscast and Political Support
Standardized Regression Coefficients (beta) controlled by socioeconomic variables (gender, education, age, income)

	Democratic Adherence					
	Disagrees w/ Government disrespecting laws in times of trouble	Prefers democra-cy than savior leader	Disagrees President should disregard Congress and Parties in times of trouble	Disagrees Country better with the return of the military	Disagrees would give a blank check to a savior leader that solved problems	Disagrees only a dictator- ship can fix Brazil
TV	-0,051***	0,059***	-0,086***	ns	-0,058***	-0,077***
TXJN	Ns	ns	Ns	ns	ns	-0,062**
R^2	0,018	0,013	0,021		0,03	0,035

	Political Community
	Proud to be Brazilian
TV	0,069***
TXJN	0,046*
R^2	0,014

	Valorization of political parties		
	Democracy has to do with the existence of various political parties	Disagrees Brazil would be better if there were only one political party	Closeness to political party
TV	Ns	-0,066***	0,088***
TXJN	Ns	ns	0,098***
R^2		0,023	0,027

Trust in Institutions

	Judiciary	Armed Forces	Congress	Federal Government	Fire department
TV	-0,048**	0,092***	0,039*	0,056***	0,084***
TXJN	Ns	0,111***	ns	0,062**	0,079***
R^2	0,022	0,035	0,028	0,03	0,035

	Police	Political parties	President	Unions	Entrepreneurs
TV	-0,060***	0,046**	0,081***	ns	-0,044*
TXJN	Ns	Ns	0,053**	ns	ns
R^2	0,024	0,021	0,058		0,024

Evaluation of Institutions

	Congressmen and Senators	Congress	Federal Government
TV	-0,048***	Ns	-0,039**
TXJN	Ns	Ns	ns
R^2	0,023		0,043

	President Lula	Political parties	President
TV	0,05***	-0,06***	ns
TXJN	Ns	Ns	ns
R^2	0,05	0,022	

Satisfaction with Democracy

tv	ns
txjn	0,049*
R^2	0,04

Significance: *$p < 0,10$, **$p < 0,05$, ***$<0,01$. Source: "Citizens' Distrust in Democratic Institutions" (2006).

In the opposite direction of TV viewership, it was expected that Brazil's main newscast fostered political support. Those who watch JN are also exposed to several other political messages on television. For instance, it seems reasonable to suppose that there is a difference between individuals who watch JN three times a week - while watching only one hour of TV a day - and another person who watches the same amount of JN, but at the same time has a four hour daily consumption of television. Thus, we used a JN viewership rate, which corresponds to the proportion of consumption of the newscast in relation to the total hours devoted to television, created by a division between JN viewership by TV viewership.

The idea here is not only a possible 'dilution' of information compared to one that is more 'pure'. It is expected that a viewer who practically restricts his TV consumption to the newscast is more attentive to its content, since he turns his TV set on with the express purpose of knowing the news of the day. However, a distinct pattern of viewership, in which the individual leaves his TV on from the period that he arrives from work until he goes to sleep - watching JN 'between the soap operas' - may indicate a less attentive pattern. This variable created proved to be a more consistent one compared to just JN viewership in a previous study (Mesquita 2010). When we speak of JN audience from now on, we are referring to this rate, i.e., always taking into account television exposure.

Where there were significant correlations, the tested models supported our hypothesis. Watching JN fosters pride in nationality, trust in institutions, valorization of political parties and satisfaction with democracy. It is not a relevant variable for evaluation of institutions or democratic adherence, with exception of one negative association with rejection of dictatorship (see Table 1).

Secondary news sources and political support: newspapers, radio and the Internet

The next set of results concerns the role that news consumption on the radio, newspapers and the Internet represent for the same dimensions presented in the former analyses. The database used was the 2008 Lapop survey. Listening to news on the radio, as expected, proved to foster political support. Although it is not a relevant variable for democratic adherence or satisfaction with democracy, it fosters greater pride in nationality, valorization of political parties, trust and positive assessments of institutions, as presented in Table 2.

Consumption of newspapers and of news on the Internet - since corresponding to a more elitist and well-informed public - was expected to foster axiological attitudes toward democracy, while increasing a more critical assessment of pragmatic dimensions of the regime. This was sustained in part. Reading newspapers does foster both valorization of political parties and a more critical assessment of institutions (trust, evaluation and satisfaction with the functioning of the regime). However, democratic adherence per se presents an ambiguous correlation. The press fosters more disapproval of censure, but at the same time undermines the idea of democracy as the best form of government. It is also related to less pride in nationality.

Table 2: Newspaper, Radio, Internet and Political Support
Standardized Regression Coefficients (beta) controlled by socioeconomic variables (gender, education, age, income)

	Democratic Adherence	
	Democracy has some problems, but is better than any other form of government	Disapproves that Government censures television programs
Newspapers	-0,076***	0,071***
Radio	ns	ns
Internet	0,104***	ns
R²	0,037	0,035

	Political community
	Proud to be Brazilian
Newspapers	-0,113***
Radio	0,108***
Internet	-0,052*
R²	0,038

	Valorization of Political Parties			
	Disagrees there can be democracy without parties	Political parties represent well their electors	Parties are close to people like me	Corruption perception in parties
Newspapers	ns	ns	0,084***	0,078***
Radio	ns	ns	0,085***	ns
Internet	ns	ns	ns	ns
R²			0,039	0,02

	Trust in Institutions					
	Entrepreneurs	Judiciary	Armed Forces	Congress	Federal Government	Unions
Newspapers	-0,056*	-0,089***	-0,066**	-0,110***	-0,139***	ns
Radio	0,046**	0,071***	0,07***	ns	0,05**	0,087***
Internet	0,073***	0,059**	ns	ns	ns	-0,114***
R²	0,025	0,055	0,038	0,036	0,056	0,039

	Military Police	Federal Police	Political parties	President	Supreme Court	Fire department
Newspapers	-0,107***	-0,114***	-0,06**	-0,106***	-0,115***	ns
Radio	0,133***	0,114***	0,046*	0,051*	0,076***	ns
Internet	ns	ns	ns	ns	ns	-0,062*
R²	0,068	0,04	0,031	0,059	0,029	0,015

Satisfaction with Democracy

Newspapers	-0,108***
Radio	ns
Internet	ns
R^2	0,042

Evaluation of Institutions

	Government promotes democratic principles	Government fights corruption	Congress makes important laws
Newspapers	-0,099***	-0,103***	-0,059**
Radio	0,09***	0,097***	0,052*
Internet	-0,068***	ns	ns
R^2	0,047	0,041	0,024
	Congress acts as expected	President Lula	Congressmen
Newspapers	ns	-0,083***	0,088***
Radio	0,057**	ns	0,103***
Internet	-0,056*	ns	ns
R^2	0,021	0,023	0,032

Significance: *p < 0,10, **p < 0,05, ***<0,01. Source: Lapop (2008).

Consumption of news on the Internet is correlated with more democratic adherence. However, the correlation with pride in nationality goes in the opposite direction, while it is not a significant variable for the dimension of valorization of political parties or satisfaction with democracy. The Internet is associated with a more critical assessment of institutions in terms of evaluation. In terms of trust, however, it depends on the institution in question. The more news consumption on the web, the more individuals trust entrepreneurs and the judiciary, and the less they trust unions and the Fire Department. Trust in most institutions, however, is not affected by this media variable.

Brief Final Considerations

The media are a relevant factor to be considered for the understanding of public affairs. The information they contain might help to engage citizens in democracy, or estrange them from democratic principles. To understand the role of the media in public support for democracy, we need to consider different impacts of various sources that citizens are exposed to.

The results presented here confirm this plural role played by the media, depending not only on the medium in question, but also on the dimensions of political support analyzed. On the one hand, even though news media in Brazil seems to be somewhat positive for political support, as the case of other countries, the picture seems a little more complex for the former. Brazil's main news source, *Jornal Nacional*, and attention to news on the radio, seem to foment a better view of democratic institutions. Although presenting politics from a critical perspective - denouncing corruption scandals - they perform a positive role presenting democratic institutions and mechanisms as a way to deal with them, which could be responsible for the positive correlation found.

On the other hand, probably because reaching a more segmented elitist public, newspaper consumption and attention to news on the Internet have a more complex picture. As predicted, these media sources are correlated with a more critical assessment of the functioning of democratic institutions. As for more axiological attitudes of political support, it is not totally positive as expected. While, for the most part, they seem to foster democratic attitudes (less so for newspapers) and valorize political parties, both media are negatively correlated with support for the political community.

The case of television also seems to be particular to the Brazilian case. In general – and as predicted – viewership is negatively associated with variables of democratic adherence and evaluation of institutions and political actors. Although more ambiguously (depending on the variable in question), it is also negatively correlated with valorization of political parties and trust in institutions. However, despite this negative role, the data also showed that television promotes greater adherence to the political community.

These results demonstrate that it is not accurate to blame an anti--political bias of the media for negative attitudes that citizens have regarding democracy. Even if a more critical attitude toward politics by news media is taken as a given, there is controversy about this representing, by extension, an anti-institutional attitude. Here, as in the case of other countries (Norris 2000, Newton 1999), news has appeared constantly as a positive factor for democratic quality.

As for television viewership, the results somehow confirm concerns about its meaning to perceptions of democracy in Brazil. Still, these results require caution, as they seem to be more associated with time spent watching television than with what is being watched. To test possible negative effects of content, more survey studies were needed with more detailed questions about specific programming. Reception studies could also be useful in this regard. In addition, we emphasize that television presents itself as a positive factor for adherence to the political community.

This result for pride in nationality could be related to the great dissemination of TV countrywide, with diffusion of common values. Taking the example of the genre of soap operas, all social classes watch this type of programming, talking about their themes and plots, which makes television act as a social bond. Representing a mirror of Brazilian society, the soaps also present themselves as a structuring factor of Brazilian identity (Wolton 1996). Thus, television can be seen as paradoxical. Although - as in other countries- it seems to be somehow tied to more negative attitudes toward politics, at the same time, in Brazil, it plays an active role - allowing the audience to build complex understandings about the past, the present and future of the country.

The argument set forward here makes the role of the media in political support a complex one. Firstly, not all media are alike. Some foster more positive political attitudes, while others seem to support the 'political disaffection' theory. Secondly, even among specific media, the roles they play are not clear-cut. They might promote some dimensions of political support, while undermining others.

Another consideration should be made regarding directionality of associations. As said before, from this type of data, it is not possible to say whether media impact political attitudes, or if citizens with certain political opinions turn to the type of media that display the worldview they already have. In this sense, it seems that different media in question might offer diverse suggestions for this relationship.

Television newscasts, as *Jornal Nacional* for example, have a more diversified audience. Many people watch it because they have their TV sets on between their favorite entertainment shows. In this case, it could be suggested of an actual positive role of the newscast, which has the potential to reach an audience previously not interested in public affairs. Conversely, the secondary sources of news analyzed here could suggest a different causal relationship. Since they are more selective in terms of consumers, it does seem plausible that they are read, listened to or watched by a public that has the same points of view these media convey. Nevertheless, a better way to understand these effects could be as a two-way flow. Although people turn to these media because they reflect certain points of view they already have, they reinforce these previous attitudes, which could be of support of democratic values, or estrangement from politics in general.

References

Almond, G. and Verba, S. (1963) *The civic culture: Political attitudes in five western democracies.* Princeton: Princeton University Press.

Cappella, J. and Jamieson, K. (1997) *Spiral of cynicism. The press and the public good.* New York/Oxford: Oxford University Press.

Chaia, V. and Teixeira, M. (2001) 'Democracia e escândalos politicos'. *São Paulo em Perspectiva*, 15(4).

Chaia, V. and Azevedo, F. (2008) 'O senado nos editoriais paulistas (2003-2004)'. *Opinião Pública*, 14(1).

Coleman, J. (1990) *Foundations of social theory.* Cambridge, MA: Harvard University Press.

'Desconfiança dos cidadãos das instituições democráticas, A', (2006) Survey of the project coordinated by professors Moisés, J. (usp) and Meneguello, R. (Unicamp), Fapesp (process: 04/07952-8).

Dalton, R. (1999) 'Political support in advanced industrial democracies' in P. Norris (ed.) *Critical citizens: Global support for democratic governance.* Oxford: Oxford University Press.

Diamond, L. and Morlino, L. (2004) 'The quality of democracy – an overview'*Journal of Democracy*, 15(4).

Easton, D. (1965) *A system analysis of political life.* New Cork: Wiley.

Inglehart, R. (2002) 'Cultura e democracia' in L. Harrison and S. Huntington, *A cultura importa – Os valores que definem o progresso humano.* Rio de Janeiro e São Paulo: Ed. Record.

Inglehart, R. and Welzel, C. (2005) *Modernization, cultural change and democracy.* New York: Cambridge University Press.

'Latin American Public Opinion Project' (2008) www.lapopsurveys.org.

Meneguello, R. (2010) 'Aspectos do desempenho democrático: Estudo sobre a adesão à democracia e avaliação do regime' in J. Moisés (ed.) *Democracia e confiança: Por que os cidadãos desconfiam das instituições públicas?.* São Paulo: Edusp.

Mesquita, N. (2010) '*Jornal Nacional*, democracia e confiança nas instituições democráticas' in J. Moisés, (ed.) *Democracia e confiança: Por que os cidadãos desconfiam das instituições públicas.* São Paulo: Edusp.

Miguel, L. (1999) 'Mídia e eleições: a campanha de 1998 na Rede Globo'. *Dados*, 42(2).

Miguel, L. (2003) 'A eleição visível: A Rede Globo descobre a política em 2002'. *Dados*, 46(2).

Miguel, L. (2004) 'Discursos cruzados: Telenoticiários, HPEG e a construção da agenda eleitoral',*Sociologias*, 6(11).

Miguel, L and Coutinho, P. (2007) 'A crise e suas fronteiras: Oito meses de mensalão nos editoriais dos jornais'. *Opinião Pública*, 13(1).

Moisés, J.(2007)'Democracy, political trust and democratic institutions (the case of Brazil)'. Paper presented in the seminar Democracy and citizens distrust of public institutions in Brazil in comparative perspectives, Oxford University, 1.º/jun./2007.

Moisés, J. (2008) 'Os Significados da democracia segundo os Brasileiros' in IV Congresso da Associação Latino-americana de Ciência Política – ALACIP, Gobernanza sin Desarrollo? Repensar el Bienestar en America Latina, Costa Rica.

Moisés, J. (2010) 'Cultura política, instituições e democracia: Lições da experiência brasileira' in J. Moisés, *Democracia e confiança: Por que os cidadãos desconfiam das instituições públicas?*. São Paulo: Edusp.

Moisés, J. and Carneiro, G. (2010) 'Democracia, desconfiança política e insatisfação com o regime – o caso do Brasil' in J. Moisés (ed.) *Democracia e confiança: Por que os cidadãos desconfiam das instituições públicas?*. São Paulo: Edusp.

Newton, K. (1999) 'Mass media effects: Mobilization or media malaise?' in *British Journal of Political Science*, 29(4).

Norris, P. (ed) (1999) *Critical citizens*, Oxford: Oxford University Press. Norris, P.(2000)*A virtuous circle: Political communications in post-industrial democracies*. Cambridge: Cambridge University Press.

North, D. (1990) *Institutions, institutional change and economic performance*. Cambridge, UK: Cambridge University Press.

Patterson, T. (1998) 'Time and news: the media's limitations as an instrument of democracy',in *International Political Science Review*, 19(1).

Patterson, T. (2000) 'The United States: news in a free-market society' in R. Gunther and A. Mughan (eds.) *Democracy and the media: A comparative perspective*. Cambridge: Cambridge University Press.

Putnam, R. (1995) 'Tuning in, tuning out: The strange disappearance of social capital in America' in *PS – Political Science and Politics*, XXVIII (4).

Porto, M. (1996) 'Televisão e voto: A eleição de 1992 para prefeito de São Paulo' in *Opinião Pública*, IV(1).

Porto, M. (2000a) 'La crisis de confianza en la política y sus instituciones: Los medios y la legitimidad de la democracia en Brasil' in *América Latina Hoy*, 25.

Porto, M. (2000b) 'Telenovelas, política e identidad nacional en Brasil' in *Ecuador Debate*, 49.

Porto, M. (2005) 'The principle of diversity in journalism:*Jornal Nacional* and political deliberation in Brazil' in *Brazilian Journalism and Research*, 1(1).

Rennó, L. (2001) 'Confiança interpessoal e comportamento político: Microfundamentos da teoria do capital social na América Latina' in *Opinião Pública*, VII(1).

Rennó, L. (2003) 'Estruturas de oportunidade política e engajamento em organizações da sociedade civil: Um estudo comparado sobre a América Latina' in *Revista de Sociologia e Política*, 21.

Schlegel, R. (2006) 'Mídia, confiança política e mobilização', Masters dissertation, fflch-usp, São Paulo.

Schmitt-Beck, R. and Voltmer, K. (2007) 'The mass media in third-wave democracies: Gravediggers ≤Democracy, intermediation, and voting on four continents*. Oxford: Oxford University Press.

Shah, D. (1998) 'Civic engagement, interpersonal trust and television use: An individual-level assessment of social capital' in *Political Psychology*, 19.

Straubhaar, J., Olsen, O. and Nunes, A. (1993) 'The Brazilian case' in T. Skidmore (ed.) *Television, politics, and the transition to democracy in Latin America*. Washington: WWC Press; Baltimore/London: JHU Press.

Uslaner, E. (1998) 'Social capital, television, and the 'mean world: Trust, optimism, and civic participation' in *Political Psychology*, 19.

Wolton, D. (1996) *Elogio do grande public*, São Paulo: Ática.

Methodological Appendix

Lapop (2008) Survey:

Independent variables:

Newspaper readership

"How often do you read newspapers (everyday, once or twice a week, rarely, never)."

News on the radio

"How often do you listen to news on the radio (everyday, once or twice a week, rarely, never)."

News on the Internet

"How often do you read or listen to news on the Internet (everyday, once or twice a week, rarely, never)."

Dependent variables:

Adherence to Democracy and Democratic Values:

"Democracy has some problems, but is better than any other form of government (Disagree a lot, 2, 3, 4, 5, 6, agree a lot)".

"With which of the following phrases do you agree more? (Democracy is preferable to any other form of government; in some circumstances an authoritarian regime may be preferable; it makes no difference if a regime is authoritarian or democratic").

"In order to arrest criminals, do you believe the authorities must always respect laws or that, in certain occasions, authorities can act without respecting laws (Must always respect laws, in certain occasions can act without respect to laws)."

"To what point do you approve or disapprove that the government censures TV programming (Totally disapprove, 2, 3, 4, 5, 6, 7, 8, 9, totally approve)"

Adherence to Political Community

"How proud are you of being Brazilian? (Not proud at all, 2, 3, 4, 5, 6, very proud)"

Adherence to political parties

"Thinking about political parties in general, how much do you agree or disagree that Brazilian political parties represent their electors well? (Disagree a lot, 2, 3, 4, 5, 6, agree a lot)"

"How much corruption is there in Brazilian political parties? (None, 2, 3, 4, 5, 6, a lot)"

"How close are political parties to people like me? (Not close at all, 2, 3, 4, 5, 6, very close)."

"There can be democracy without political parties (Disagree a lot, 2, 3, 4, 5, 6, agree a lot)."

"How much trust do you have in political parties (None, 2, 3, 4, 5, 6, a lot)."

Evaluation of Institutions

"Up to what point would you say (not at all, 2, 3, 4, 5, 6, a lot): 'Congress passes laws and policies important to the country'; 'Congress corresponds to what is expected from it'; 'The Federal Government fights corruption'; 'The Federal Government promotes and protects democratic principles'."

"And speaking in general about the current Government, how do you evaluate the work President Lula has been doing?" (Very bad, bad, neither good nor bad, good, very good)

"Do you think congressmen are doing a (Very bad, bad, neither good nor bad, good or very good) work?"

Satisfaction with Democracy

"Generally speaking, are you very satisfied, satisfied, dissatisfied, very dissatisfied with the functioning of democracy in Brazil?"

Institutional Trust

"Up to what point do you trust (not at all, 2, 3, 4, 5, 6, a lot): entrepreneurs, the judiciary, the armed forces, Congress, Federal Government, unions, military police, federal police, political parties, The President, supreme court, fire department"

"Citizens' Distrust in Democratic Institutions" (2006) Survey: Independent variables:

TV viewership

"How many hours a day do you spend watching TV (up to 1, 2, 3, 4, 5 hours, more than 5 hours? Or you do not usually watch TV?)"

Jornal Nacional viewership

"How often do you watch TV Globo's Jornal Nacional during the week? (1, 2, 3, 4, 5 times, every day or you never watch JN?) "

Dependent variables:

Adherence to Democracy and Democratic Values:

Would you say you (strongly disagree, somewhat disagree, somewhat agree, strongly agree):

"When there is a difficult situation in Brazil, it doesn't matter if the Government disregards laws, the Congress and institutions to solve the problems of the country."

"I Prefer Democracy rather than a savior leader who has all power, without being controlled by laws"

"If the country is facing serious difficulties, the President may disregard parties and Congress and make decisions alone"

"The country would be better off if the military returned to power"

"I'd give a blank check to a savior leader to solve the problems of the country"

"Only a dictatorship can fix Brazil"

Adherence to Political Community

"Are you proud of being Brazilian? (Not proud at all, a little proud, proud, very proud)"

Adherence to political parties

"Speaking of the Brazilian political parties, how do you feel about them?" (Very close, close, somewhat close, not close to any "
"Brazil would be better off if there were only one political party"

"Speaking of democracy, do you think democracy has to do with: the existence of several political parties" (has much to do, has to do, has little to do, has nothing to do)

Evaluation of Institutions

I would like you to say what is your evaluation – very good, good, neither good nor bad, bad or very bad - of each one of the following institutions: a) the army; b) the judiciary power; c) police; d) the

National Congress; e) the political parties; f) the Government; g) the President.

Satisfaction with Democracy

"Would you say that you are very satisfied, satisfied, not very satisfied, or not at all satisfied with the functioning of democracy in Brazil?"

Institutional Trust

"I am going to mention now some public institutions and would like to know what is the degree of trust that you have for each one of them: a lot, some, a little or not trust at all: a) the army, b) the firemen, c) judiciary power, d) president, e) police, f) government, g) National Congress, h) political parties and

"I am going to mention now some private institutions and would like to know what is the degree of trust that you have in each one of them: a lot, some, a little or not trust at all": the unions, the entrepreneurs"

CHAPTER 2

NEWS COVERAGE, POLITICAL COMMUNICATION, CRISIS AND CORRUPTION IN PORTUGAL

Isabel Ferin Cunha

Preamble

The coverage of political communication in Western democracies has undergone great mutations in recent decades due both to technological factors and changes in media, economic, political and social systems. One of the most decisive factors has been the increasing centrality of the Media and the consequent need of the political system to adapt to this reality. Among the strategies adopted is the delivery of political communication management to political advisers, and other professionals like spin doctors who tend to administer the relationship between politicians (and govern-ments) and citizens through a logic of "attracting and persuading audiences." This phenomenon determines the mobilization of all resources in order to weaken the opponents; these include: rumors, allegations or suspicions of corruption. On the other hand, the pressure on Media companies to make profits and increase their audiences tends towards the scheduling of certain political issues, such as charges of corruption; given their potential to shock this then leads them to increased audiences (Allern and Pollack 2012: 9-28). If we add to this a crisis scenario, not only economic, but also include democratic values, then the importance of reflecting upon all these factors together can be understood.

DOI: http://dx.doi.org/10.14195/978-989-26-0917-1_2

Within this context, we will characterize the coverage in Western democracies and relate that coverage to changes in political communication as well as develop the coverage of political corruption within a crisis scenario.

Contexts of news and political communication

The representation of political corruption by the Media in Western democracies is intrinsically related to the characteristics of news coverage of political communication. Political communication has a horizontal dimension that consists of the relationships between politicians and the Media, and a vertical dimension involving political institutions as a whole, and also politicians and their relationships with citizens (Blumler and Gurevitch 1995). This Media triangle involves political players, businesses and Media professionals and citizens, the latter regarded as audiences.

McNair (1999) outlines the flow of political communication and begins by listing the political organizations and political interests involved, such as parties, public organizations, governments and pressure groups. Following on from this he refers to the area of the Media, stressing that they act on the basis of economic affiliations and advertising agencies, depending upon technological and human resources, as well production routines and audience targets. The final part in the chain of political communication flow is the public, who are not only the recipients but also the weakest link, voting at elections as a means of response. Meanwhile, the progressive replacing of the principle of mediation in political communication by the principle of mediatisation, has resulted in the penetration of values inherent in the Media sphere in political life (Mazzoleni and Schulz 1999, Meyer 2002).

This process began in Europe in the eighties, as a result of the development of new technologies and market liberalisation policies which gradually led to the commoditisation of journalistic information. This evolution has had consequences on the news coverage of political phenomena, as well as on political communication strategies, resulting in the so-called 'Americanisation' of politics, distinguished by the introduction of aspects arising from advertising and markets (Blumler and Gurevitch 1982, 1995, 2000, Fergusen 1990, Semetetko and all. 1992, Franklin 1994). Patterson (2003: 22), referring to the evolution of American journalism over the latter decades of the 20th century, notes that the number of 'serious' news items has decreased, while 'light' news has been on the increase. This has meant that the news involving political coverage, political communication and relevant public policy issues, that is: serious news, has given way to other light news, which itself has tended towards sensationalism, and what is more was deemed as being out of context with regard to time and space. Furthermore, this has led to greater focus on matters centred on a particular character, unrelated to public policies.

The decrease in appearance time in the Media (sound bites) has generated the belief in politicians and the politicized elite, that there is a progressive distortion in the quality of the policy, which is further increased by a declining ability on the part of politicians to reach the public at large. In response to this situation, policy-makers have focused upon political marketing and aggressive strategies of political persuasion in order to impose themselves in the Media and reach the electorate more effectively. Moreover, since politicians verbal messages are often truncated, shortened and framed by journalists, the images of politicians tend to acquire greater significance (Grabe 2009: 54). With these assumptions and in order to reach the public and overcome the constraints identified in the Media, especially on television, governments and parties tend to choose leaders and candidates with greater personal potential in the Media.

The process of political personalization is a political response to the difficulties that governments and political parties face when appealing to citizens and voters, but it is also a strategy that calls attention to the building of Media personalities as celebrities. The public image of governments and candidates is always portrayed to include qualities such as trust, authority and security. However, the credibility of political actors also depends upon what aspects of their private life have become public, such as moral and physical appearance: oral proficiency (speaking well, using the right word at the right time); a fitting image (calm appearance, appropriate dress); credibility (keeping promises) and reputation (honesty, integrity and probity).

Within the context described, politics involves new players, who are preferably located backstage in governance and political campaigns (Louw 2005). These players are highly skilled professionals such as those found in marketing companies, experts in public policy, political advisers (spin doctors), journalists and political commentators (pundits and opinion makers). These professionals are characterized by being specialized in technical and communication strategies, and by lacking in any party affiliation and party loyalty. The arrival of these experts into politics has led to the increased complexity of political relationships within Western democracies, and also the position of players in defining the political game.

On the other hand, the role that these actors assume in the daily life of party politics and governance, has resulted in the proliferation of information "wars" focusing upon the strategies of political advisers, in order to impose "favourable opinion" in the public sector (Maarek 2007). The struggle to establish the most favourable attitude of either a particular political agent, or issue, in both the political field and in public opinion, involves the ability to establish, throughout the media, political agendas imposing the notion of "how to think" (Meraz 2011). Being visible in the Media and getting the general public out of politics, leads to the use of multiple Media (traditional and W.2) and multiple communication strategies, which include the use of accusations of corruption that may remove legitimacy from potential opponents (Fladmoe and Jenssen 2012: 53-71)

The reporting of cases of alleged corruption and scandals in the Media which give rise, without justification, to proving the culpability of the politicians involved also contributes to discrediting democracy, as well as the political system itself and its agents. Simultaneously, the complaint or even the mere suggestion of such scenarios even existing has constituted to one of the great weapons of political struggle: allowing the patrimony of a politician, within a highly personalized system, based on his/her image and reputation, to be eroded immediately. Thus, these type of complaints are one of the most common ways to neutralize opposition candidates and promote "the settling of scores" in the public arena. Moreover, such strategies feed the Media industry by encouraging the production and consumption of news and giving more power and visibility to the Media.

According to Allern and Pollack (2012: 9-28) the Media coverage of these issues would be associated with increased competition between traditional and online Media, the need to capture audiences, establish schedules and save resources and also with promoting political transgressions in a sensationalistic way. It is also linked to the ever growing divide between the demands of public codes of behaviour and the practices of individual politicians as well as the strategies of political advisers to annihilate opponents and maintain control of political agendas.

The political field involves, therefore, complex processes of information management and communication, along with specific skills and competencies in the management of human resources and technology. The strategic objective is the control of agendas and impression management in the mainstream Media, especially television, where politicians are more often exposed and are forced to adopt a profile. As a complement, the advisors and public relations staff, the men behind scenes, have to closely monitor client image adjustment, drawing on the help of regular polls.

The abovementioned American and European trend would be echoed in Portugal, some decades later. This delay was due to various reasons, such as the late introduction of a Media market and the consequent results of this change on social practices and policies (Serrano 2006, Cunha 2006, Jalali 2007). In Portugal, after a decade-long expansion in the Media and advertising fields, the economic and financial crisis led to a market crunch. In reaction to this situation, the corporate groups who were running the printed Media, television broadcasts and *online* Media sought to generate synergies, aiming at lowering production costs. Thus, major restructuring in newsrooms took place, with the goal of amalgamating news production centres. At the same time, human resources were optimised, with journalists and other professionals being faced with growing levels of job insecurity, while flexibility in work hours increased, and a growing number of tasks were given to freelancers, daily workers and interns (Garcia 2010). The migration of advertising, which due to the economic crisis had already been reduced to subscription-based television channels and digital Media, brought about yet further constraints to Portuguese journalism.

While economic and professional factors have limited the action of News Media in recent decades, resulting in 'inexpensive' and profit-centred journalism, like the *News of the World*, for instance, it is no less true that there remains a need to keep audiences involved in transforming the news into a show of their own. The news as entertainment and entertainment-information alone hardly poses any serious threat to democracy (McNair 1999). In fact, this type of coverage, when associated with political speeches rooted in the principle of credibility, may even garner greater visibility for political communication, drawing a large section of the public, traditionally oblivious of public issues, to participate in public debate and, therefore, in democracy (Brants 1998). However, as Patterson noted (1994), a sensationalist and commercial approach to political information tends to boost populism, contributing to the politicisation of journalism and emphasising the backstage of politics.

This set of trends in news coverage, on the one hand, results in 'tabloidisation' (Esser 1999) of political communication and increasing alienation of ordinary citizens from the political field, while, on the other, it encourages the emergence of a new audience standard, marked by fragmentation, volatility and an absence of any ideological affiliation which seeks to fill in the lack of political information by resorting to alternative means (Atkinson 2009). While the former audiences focus preferably on generalist broadcasters, the latter focus on *online* vehicles in their search for information that might differ from the ordinary menu offered by traditional media (Morgan 2011). The intersection of the two latter trends with aggressive political communication strategies, involving elements of pop culture, has generated an increase of distrust in representative democracy, demonstrated by growing alienation of citizens from electoral acts (Wolton 2008).

To those constraints, a common feature in most Western democratic societies, one must add specific aspects that pertain to Portuguese society. Among these, one can mention the traditional promiscuity between journalism's elite and politicians, and also between journalists and the judicial sector. This adds to a clear rotation among party members and sympathisers in carrying out their public duties and in occupying governmental seats, as well as holding executive positions in large economic groups, both in the public and private sectors (Morgado e Vegar 2003, Moreira e Silva 2008, Costa, Fazenda, Honório, Rosas e Louçã 2010, *Transparencia e Integridade* Report 2011).

We must also emphasise the interest groups that are associated with Media companies, who put party and political pressure on these companies and also the shortage of news-worthy raw material and its ability to generate audiences. The State, or specifically the Government, has been seen to exert control over the private Media through institutional advertising, as well as through criteria imposed by regulatory agencies of communication. All these factors influence news coverage of the potential phenomena of corruption, in addition to aspects of the political arena, such as political marketing strategies by parties and members of Government, competitive phenomena in the political market, politicians' images, perception of dominant and emerging values and campaigns of disinformation and damage control (Maarek 1997, Lees-Marshment 2011).

Framing crisis and corruption

Etymologically, the word originates from *krisis*, Greek for separation, dispute, decision, verdict or final decision. *Crisis* in Latin means change, sudden imbalance; state of doubt and uncertainty; tension, conflict (Cunha 1982: 228). Norberto Bobbio, in his "Political Dictionary" (2004: 303-306), defines crisis as a moment of breach in a system, and considers that crises can be distinguished by three elements: unpredictability, limited duration, and impact on the functioning of the system.

To understand a crisis it is necessary to take into account the internal and external contexts that predate it, as well as the changes in the system that have originated it. In the stage of crisis itself, one must dedicate special attention to the issues of time and space involved in any crisis and to the actors and protagonists at stake. Bobbio considers that political and economic crises are inextricably connected, both at national and international level, as demonstrated by the international economic crisis of 1929-1932 that had severe repercussions on domestic political systems. Thus, crises can originate from inside or outside the system; they evolve according to a peak, which means that over the course of a crisis, other crises may overlap, causing overloads in political, economic, legal and social systems. For example, the financial crisis that is currently felt across the whole of Europe has had several internal crises and peaks, which have resulted in ups and down in stock markets, in credit rating scares and in the measures adopted by EU member states.

The same author also distinguishes crises in a system from Government and international crises. A system crisis is associated with change of political regime, as well as with changes in legal and constitutional mechanisms and devices, as for example in the end of a Monarchy and the establishment of a Republic, or at the end of a dictatorial regime and the introduction of democracy. Still within the topic of system crisis, we also find transformation of socio-economic relations – including such aspects as production relations, distribution of wealth and income and the notion of family (Bobbio, Matteuci e Pasquino 2004: 304). It should be noted that the two aspects are deeply interlinked, which means it is impossible for any change in regime not to bring about change to socio--economic relations, or for socio-economic changes to occur without a substantial change in the philosophy and design of a regime. Government crises are related to the operation of the Government subsystem and may originate from internal factors inherent to the context and governmental structure, or external factors pertaining to relations with society or with aspects resulting from unfavourable international situations. The author points out that one of the decisive factors of any Government crisis may result from the relations between the politicians' class and society and may depend on "the lack of representativeness of the political class in power".

The institutionalisation of procedures with a view to solving Government crises mostly aims to control the damage that could affect the regime

(Bobbio, Matteuci e Pasquino 2004: 305). These reflections, applied to the current situation in many European countries, lead to urgent questioning on citizenship and the very future of representative democracy.

International crises arise from conflicts between countries. Historically, the concept has always been always associated with conflicts, wars and the hegemonic ambitions of certain countries. According to Bobbio, Matteuci, Pasquino (2004: 305), there is a huge advantage in analysing international crises from the point of view of the available information, the quality and number of actors involved, the decision-making processes and the results achieved.

An exercise that might actually be useful for the current situation in Europe is the analysis of journalistic coverage of the financial crisis. While undertaking this exercise one quickly identifies a small number of customised active, players, a profuse circulation of data and statistics, as well as few actual measures that could lead to a solution for the problem. Within this context journalistic coverage by the Media adopts the power of speech of interest groups represented within the State, which through economic, financial and legal devices, encourages citizens to conform to vague interests, mostly financial in nature, of national and global scope (Nash 2005). This process can be described, to a large extent, by managing the voices that reach the public arena and to whom the Media lends the floor, for example: the collective players 'markets', 'banks', 'financial markets', 'the rich', G20, G8, or even singling out certain countries of particular geostrategic interest. Citizens are merely viewed as passive and reactive players, and identified as 'employees', 'contributors', 'civil servants', 'the retired', 'users of public services'. The voice of the trade unions and union federations is also passive or reactive in relation to the decisions made by the active players, as well as the 'demonstrators', 'rioters' or the 'outraged'.

The deficit of representation in the public sphere, as sensed by the majority of citizens in various regions of the globe and a growing suspicion toward the informative menu administered by Media companies, have given rise to social movements with diverse goals. Examples of such movements include for instance: the anti-dictatorship movements that broke out in North African countries; the movement of 'the outraged' against the austere remedies aimed at tackling the financial crisis in Europe, or even the 'Occupy Wall Street' movement in the United States, who are opposed to the practices of financial systems. All these movements hold in common the use of online tools and social networks, as well as a specific strategy to change the dominant discourse of public space, demanding new criteria of 'truth' and 'credibility' (Atkinson 2009).

To Raboy and Dagenais (1992: 2-5) crises are of great interest to the Media, not only because they provide an opportunity to challenge the political system, the opponent or powerful partner, but also due to the economic advantages that such situations can bring to companies, as they generally bring about an increase in available raw material for news-making and a growing demand from citizens/consumers. These same authors also consider that a tendency of the Media for fabricating or emphasising crises is traceable, and that they include procedures which tend to be consistent with powerful interests and actors. Underneath this statement lies the conclusion (Keane 1992: 20-21) that Western democracies have created a system of dangerous relations between the political class, businesses, Media and journalists, allowing less than clear situations to occur.

These observations suggest that boundaries between the State and the interests of certain powerful groups have become increasingly blurred, as certain unscrutinised powers emerge, bringing influence and various forms of corruption which mine the system from within. On the other hand, and at the same time, democratic political systems, when faced with crisis situations, tend to adopt safety measures that include the introduction of restrictions on Media activities, and control over the news sources and agendas. One example of this being the measures adopted by the mayor of New York on the accreditation of journalists dispatched to cover the 'Occupy Wall Street' protests, which tended to limit the freedom of information.

The crisis is also a type of discourse on public affairs in the public arena, involving specific codes, where the focus is on certain types of narrative, certain sources, actors and opinion makers. The crisis discourse resorts to persuasion and intimidation devices centred upon a coherent set of meanings, seeking to reflect the interests and ideological choices of very specific sectors of society. Under these circumstances the conventional Media have been playing a role of amplifying elite voices and choices, conditioning the public areas of debate by the participation of opinion makers and political leaders affiliated with the dominant system (Couldry 2010). In the financial crisis that began in 2007, with the collapse of Lehman Brothers, and in the years that followed, the voices on the public stage have been sponsoring a veritable "pensée unique" centred on the conformed and conformist vision of the causes of financial crisis. Since then, the Western Media have encouraged journalistic coverage of the financial crisis solely tending toward the exaltation of the interests of capital, as formed within the 'markets', and the punishment of economy and labour.

Moreover, crises also cause an escalation of social demands, which in turn lead the political and economic actors and agents to limit political and civil rights, notably through control over information. This control is conducted by overlooking transient micro and macro-political aspects of the crisis, through processes of ideological guidance of speech about the economic and financial situation, added to simultaneous strategies of concealment and by manipulating information in the public domain. Regarding the current financial crisis, it is of the utmost importance to analyse how focused journalistic coverage is on global financial interests, hiding the economic and social consequences of the so-called 'austerity measures' imposed, for instance, in many countries of Southern Europe.

The devices of 'spectacularisation' and the 'hyper- media-exploitation' of events and actors are discursive strategies of development of the political, economic and financial crisis (Bruck 1992: 109-110). Some of the most frequent discursive strategies are: the exhaustive and controlled presentation of information fragments contained in sound bytes; resorting to such scenarios as conferences or summits; customising public and institutional contexts; the denial of macro-contexts and direct culprits; the control of opinions and voices who have access to the public stage and the option for moralistic frameworks. These criteria incorporated into journalistic coverage by the press and television news programmes limit the public's understanding of the crisis, make the understanding of macro-contexts and alternative solutions more difficult and bring about breaches in social cohesion, solidarity among citizens and countries as well as the strengthening of moralistic speeches with xenophobic tendencies.

Within the Portuguese Media, references to the crisis have been constant since the beginning of the millennium. Empirical studies on the coverage of the final periods in Prime Ministers' terms (Cavaco Silva, 1994-1995; António Guterres, 2001-2002; Santana Lopes, 2004-2005) by the recognised press note the recurring frequency of topics such as deficit, economy, crisis and corruption (Ferin Cunha 2006: 30-38). In a subsequent empirical study about the 2009 legislative elections, the concern for the issues pertaining to 'the crisis' and 'corruption' was once again confirmed (Ferin Cunha 2012). Thus, by analysing the press, one can conclude that the second most focused upon theme was 'economy, finance and crisis' (19.9%, 208 out of 1043), and the fourth most: 'Scandals and lawsuits' (5.4%, 56 out of 1043). Meanwhile, on subscription-based television channels, out of a total number of 630 records, the themes 'Scandals and lawsuits' (9.7%, 61 mentions) and 'Economy, finance and crisis' (4.9%, 31 mentions) hold, respectively, the third and fourth highest placed mentions, within the context of the coverage of elections.

Political corruption

Rose-Ackerman (1999), discussing crisis and corruption, concluded that crises generate political, economic, social and moral changes. Firstly, the phenomenon results in the alienation of citizens from their rulers and tends to generate de-politicisation in the public sphere, paving the way for diminished perceived legitimacy of the political system and institutions. Secondly, in contemporary history, crises display mainly economic and financial characteristics that involve defrauding the expectations of citizens and societies, and clearly contribute to the increase in corruption phenomena, in their many forms.

Dobel (1978) considers that corruption greatly results from the sparse amount of goods available at a given time in a given society, which tends to bring out a sense of 'struggle for survival' coupled with a lowering in civic and ethical standards. For this author, political corruption is a phenomenon historically inherent to crisis contexts and to the final breaths of regimes, and is always associated, in the West, to the legitimacy crises, where actors (citizens and politicians) qualify the political order as corrupt and undertake actions aimed at overthrowing it.

Gambetta (2002) argues that, in common language, corruption carries several notions, of which three are the most important. According to one idea, corruption pertains to the degradation of the (public or private) agents' sense of ethics, implying a lack of moral integrity and consequent depravation. From another perspective, corruption can be associated with a set of social practices stemming from the degradation of some institutions (public or private), its focus therefore lying on institutional relations and the organization of society. A third view of corruption highlights certain social practices, with strong cultural overtones, such as gifts, etc., in order to encourage or reward certain decisions from public or private agents.

The broadest definition of corruption regards the misappropriation of assets or gains, while further elaboration on the concept leads to three main scenarios: a first, where the degradation of the involved parties' sense of ethics occurs; a second, with a set of predatory social practices within certain institutions; and the third scenario, where institutions and agents agree on misappropriation of benefits (Heidenheimer and Johnston 2002: 3-73). The wrongdoings classified as corruption are diverse in nature, including 'gifts', 'gloves', 'back-handers', clientele relations, kleptocracy, nepotism, misappropriation of benefits, white collar crime, organised crime.

The social perception of corruption involves elements of local and national culture, as the notion of what is legitimate and legal differs both from time to time and from one country to another. For example, in some countries, donations to parties are completely unlawful, but not in others and, under certain circumstances, are actually acceptable: "In Italy the socialist argued that the bribes they took were for their party rather than for personal gain, and that, since there is no other way for them to finance their electoral campaigns, donations should be legalized "(Gambetta 2002: 34).

To elaborate further: political corruption can be defined as an abuse of power for one's own benefit undertaken by democratically elected political agents. This situation may occur while carrying out public duties, or afterwards, when politicians use the relative capital acquired during their terms of office for obtaining undue gains. The wrongdoings primarily occur in four typical situations: in the course of running for political office, in the exercise of public office, while legislating or ruling, as well as after stepping down from political positions while still in charge of certain political duties in one's party (Heidenheimer and Johnston 2002).

Political corruption is a crossroads between politics (power), the economy (companies and businesses), justice (the legal framework) and Media (the disclosure of information) (Blankenburg 2002). La Porta and Méry (1997), Blankenburg (2002), Philp (2002), Bobbio consider that privatisation carried out within European territory, extended in the 1980s and 1990s, has contributed to the increase in corruption. They underline, firstly, that the financial and economic paradigm shift favoured certain already well-established interest groups, who have enjoyed increased privileges. Those groups have devised strategies, such as alternating managers between public and private-sector positions, aimed at exerting influence on governmental decisions.

Donatella de La Porta and Ives Méry (1997) have demonstrated that from the late 1990s onward, there has been an increase in the signs that suggest a rise in corrupt practices in Western democracies; to such an extent that a phenomenon which was previously deemed sporadic by the public came to be regarded as truly endemic. The increased perception of corruption, mostly political, in Western societies and most notably in Southern European countries, such as Spain, Portugal and Greece, are connected to political changes initiated throughout the 1990s, with the accession of those countries to the EEC. Political change, the financial and the economic expansion and growth of consumer society, resulted in the emergence of a new ruling elite. This group, mostly of rural origin and a notable newcomer to politics, combined traditional political practices, such as cronyism and nepotism, with capitalist and consumer society values, adopting power strategies rooted in economic and financial interests. The most frequent types of political corruption thus arise in the form of fraud, bribery, cronyism, misappropriation of gains, trafficking of influences, arbitrary favouring and illegal funding of political parties.

In Portugal, the disclosure of political corruption phenomena started in the nineties and as some studies have shown (Paixão 2010) was associated with the emergence of a Media market, supported by private television operators and new ways of practising journalism. However, the phenomena of political corruption rose to particular prominence during the 17th (March 12, 2005 to October 26, 2009) and 18th (October 26, 2009 to June 21, 2011) Constitutional Governments, led by the Socialist Party under the leadership of Prime Minister José Sócrates. During this period, between 2006 and 2009, Portugal dropped from 26th to 35th place in the international ranking on public perception of corruption conducted by Transparency International.

Disclosure and transparency: an inconclusive conclusion

Amidst an adverse situation in Western democracies, where the ordinary citizen tends to view politics as some sort of agency aimed at administrating the interests of capital and finance, the speeches on disclosure and transparency have earned increasingly symbolic value (Avritzer, Gignotto, Guimarães e Starling 2008). Both processes rely on common devices, such as scenarios, roles and legal discourses, regardless of the actions that take place in public arenas covered by the Media. The goal of these procedures is to establish the 'truth', identify the 'lie' and punish the 'guilty'. The interests of the Media, journalists and judges converge, as they all face a political system of hidden powers and fight against certain interests fiercely established within the State. The former, in contexts of economic and financial crisis, can make profits from the presentation of corruption as raw material, as well as from the subsequent 'judicialisation' of politics. In turn, justice may regard the Media and journalists as potential allies capable of overcoming the slow paced mechanisms of legal bureaucracy and of disarming pressures from within the political arena.

However, while the judge appears before the eyes of ordinary people as a punisher whose action is hindered by obligations and codes, the journalist apparently seems to enjoy greater freedom, guided by a representation of justice that transcends the boundaries of the institution. This public perception of justice allows the Media to take up the role of intermediary between powers, sometimes playing the role of accuser, sometimes defence lawyer, and other times playing judge, in cases where news potential is greatest. In these cases, violations of confidentiality during investigations are also frequent, as they are often promoted by the Media, by reporting on information obtained from judicial sources, creating partial knowledge of the facts, usually referred to as "hypothetical information", and encouraging trials by the public.

This way, the Media becomes a permanent stage for speeches on disclosing corruption, where the 'truth' is established and constantly re-established through moral discourses and legal arguments. In this context, political marketing and political communication play a crucial role in the design and survey of scenarios, in creating strategies for political agents and in exerting control over discourses about the 'truth'. Resorting to disclosure and denunciation not only affects the political actors, by delegitimizing their actions, but also promotes discredit and distrust in representative democracy as a whole.

While disclosure processes follow their courses, calls for government transparency arise in order to strengthen confidence in democracy. Lindstedt and Naurin (2010) contend that merely making information accessible or enacting legislation on corruption is not enough. The same authors consider that measures adopted by governments and public officials aiming to make institutions more transparent are less likely to actually apply to, or successfully tackle, the problem than the initiatives which are embraced by the public. Generalised distrust in measures adopted by Governments/States is rooted in the perception that there are two types of transparency: the one controlled by the information producer (the actor who produces the information and accepts the responsibility for its publication) and the other that is not controlled by the producing agent, *i.e.* the information that is published by someone other than those who are producing it, with no involvement in the process. The first form of transparency is more likely to prove ineffective, resulting in merely formal transparency procedures.

These statements serve the purpose of highlighting the decisive role of the public in the fight against corruption, in particular through awareness of the damage caused to representative democracy and the economy. In order for transparency to serve as an actual means of preventing political corruption it is necessary to make information available to citizens, alerting them to the scale of the crimes as well as to the alleged offenders, thus inhibiting their criminal conduct. However, in order for institutions to be more transparent, for broader levels of participation to be reached and for civic responsibility to be improved, radical change in the notion of democracy and democratic participation is required.

A more advanced level of participatory democracy is therefore necessary, one that might bring together new actors and forms of political communication, using the Media and alternative political contents, and able to break the domination of Western representative democracies that hold obscure interests lodged within their very cores.

References

Avritzer, L. , Gignotto, N., Guimarães, J. e Starling, H. M. M. (org.) (2008) *Corrupção: Ensaios e críticas*, Belo Horizonte, Editora UFMG.

Blankenburg, E. (2002) 'From political clientelism to outright corruption — The rise of the scandal industry' in S. Kotkin and A. Sajó (eds.) *Political corruption in transition: A skeptic's handbook*, Budapeste, Central European University Press.

Bobbio, N., Matteuci, N. e Pasquino, G. (2004) *Dicionário de política*, Brasília, Universidade de Brasília.

Campus, D. (2010) ´Mediatization and Personalization of Politics in Italy and France: The cases of Berlusconi and Sarkozy', *The International Journal of Press Politics*, 15: 219-235.

Charron, N. (2009) 'The impact of socio-political integration and press freedom on corruption´, *Journal of Development Studies*, 39 (4): 1-21.

Costa, J., Fazenda, L., Honório, C., Rosas, F., Louçã, F. (2010) *Os donos de Portugal*, Porto, Afrontamento.

Couldry, N. (2010) *Why voices matters: Culture and politics after neoliberalism*, London, Sage.

Cunha, A. G. da (1982) *Dicionário etimológico da língua portuguesa*, São Paulo, Nova Fronteira.

Della Porta, D. and Meny, Y. (1997) *Democracy and corruption in Europe*, London, Observatoire du Changement en Europe Occidental.

Dobel, J. P. (1978) 'The corruption of the state', *American Political Science Review*, 72 (3): 958-973.

Edelman, M. (1976) *The symbolic uses of politics*, Champaign, University of Illinois Press.

Esser, F., Pfetsch, B. (2004) *Comparing political communication: theories, cases and challenges*, Cambridge, University Press.

Ferin Cunha, I. (coord.) *Jornalismo e Democracia*, Lisboa, Paulus.

Ferin Cunha, I. (2012) A cobertura televisiva de partidos, candidatos e temas nas legislativas in R. Figueiras (ed.) *Os Media e as eleições: Europeias, legislativas e autárquicas*, Lisboa, Universidade Católica Editora.

Gambetta, D. (2002) ´Corruption: An analytical map' in S. Kotkin and A. Sajó (eds.)*Political corruption in transition: a skeptic's handbook*, Budapeste, Central European University Press.

Garcia, J. L. (2010) ´Para o estado da arte da investigação sobre os jornalistas portuguesas´, *Revista Media & Jornalismo*, 9 (2): 125-150.

Heidenheirmer, A. J. and Johnston, M. (ed.) (2002) *Political corruption: Concepts & contexts* (3ed.), New Jersey, The State University.

Jacobs, J. B. (2002) ´Dilemmas of corruption control' in S. Kotkin and A. Sajó (eds.) *Political corruption in transition: A skeptic's handbook*, Budapeste, Central European University Press.

Jalali, C. (2007) *Partidos e democracia em Portugal*, Lisboa: ICS.

Jenssen, A. T., Fladmoe, A. (2012) 'Ten commandements for the scandalization of political opponents' in S. Allern and E. Pollack (eds.) *Scandalous !: The mediated construction of political scandals in four nordic countries*, Gothenbourg, University of Gothenburg.

Kotkin, S. and Sajó, A. (eds.) (2002) *Political corruption in transition:A skeptic's handbook*, Budapeste, Central European University Press.

Leblanc, G. (1997) `Del modelo judicial a los procesos mediáticos' in G. Gauthier y J. Mouchon (eds.) *Comunicacion y politica*, Barcelona, Gedisa.

Lees-Marshment, J. (2011) *Political marketing: Principles and applications*, Park Square, Routledge.

Lindstedt, C. and Naurin, D. (2009) 'Transparency is not enough: Making transparency effective in reducing corruption´ *International Political Science Review,*31 (3): 301-322.

Maarek, P. J. (2007) *Communication & marketing de l´homme politique*, Paris, LexisNexis Litec.

Meraz, S. (2011) 'The fight for "how to think": Traditional media, social networks, and issue interpretation´ *Journalism*, 12 (1): 107-127.

Meyer, T. (2002) *Media democracy: How the media colonize politics*, Cambridge, Polity Press.

Morgado, D. e Silva, P. (2008)´Recompensas dos altos cargos: Portugal uma perspectiva comparada´, *IV Congresso da Associação Portuguesa de Ciência Política*.

Morgado, M. J. e Vegar, J. (2003) *Fraude e corrupção em Portugal: O inimigo sem rosto*, Lisboa, Publicações D. Quixote.

Paixão, B. (2010) *O Escândalo político em Portugal*, Coimbra, Minerva.

Philp, M. (2002) ´Political corruption, democratization, and reform´in S. Kotkin and A. Sajó (eds.) *Political Corruption in transition: A skeptic's handbook*, Budapeste, Central European University Press.

Raboy, M. and Dagenais, B. (1992) *Media, crisis and democracy*, London, Sage.

Report Transparência e Integridade (2011) Sistema Nacional de Integridade, Lisboa, Transparência Internacional/ICS.

Shea, D. (1999) All scandal politics is local: ethical lapses, the Media and congressional elections, *International Journal of Press Politics*, 4:45-62.

Serrano, E. (2006) *Jornalismo político em Portugal: a cobertura de eleições presidenciais na imprensa e na televisão (1976-2001)*, Lisboa, Ed. Colibri.

Sousa, L. de e Triães, J. (2007) *Corrupção e ética em democracia: o caso de Portugal*, Lisboa, ObercomBrief.

Thompson, J. B. (2002) *O escândalo político: poder e visibilidade na era mídia*, Rio de Janeiro, Vozes.

Transparency International (2005) *Global report 2004: Political corruption*, Cambridge, University Press.

Wolton, D. (2008) La communication politique: construction d'un modèle in *La Communication Politique*, Paris, CNRS.

CHAPTER 3
DEMOCRATIC CULTURE, PUBLIC OPINION AND PUNDITRY IN PORTUGAL

Rita Figueiras

Introduction

The integration of Portugal in the European Union in 1986 prompted a vast transformation to the country, namely modernization, and political stability (Braga da Cruz 1995). These changes had a huge impact on Portuguese economic structures (higher income rates and a progressive internationalization of the Portuguese economy), employment (socio--professional change, feminization and progressive growth in the tertiary sector), education and qualification of the Portuguese population (particularly amongst young generations and women), democratization of political structures, and liberalization of the media sector (Freire 2003, Cardoso and Costa 2005). Hence, in the aftermanth of both the institutionalization of Portuguese democracy and the development of the media sector in the 1990s, an increased relevance given to public debate started to be noticed, and, with that, the value and visibility given to punditry increased considerably (Figueiras 2005, 2008, 2011).

The valorization of public debate culture can be framed in western societies' cultural matrix, which perceives democracy as a social organization model structured itself around communication and public opinion as the prime mover of democratic politics (Habermas 1984, Fraser 1991,

DOI: http://dx.doi.org/10.14195/978-989-26-0917-1_3

2007, Luhmann 1992, Schudson 1995). In several instances within the public sphere, where the media and op-ed pages represent the 'public voice' of the press (Nimmo and Combs 1993, McNair 2003), society debates public issues and public opinion is built.

Jürgen Habermas and Niklas Luhmann are leading scholars whose theories embody opposite archetypes regarding public opinion function in democratic politics. For Habermas (1984), it is through communication that debate takes place in society, and where citizens embody a powerful political role in reinforcing civic culture. Diversity and pluralism of voices, themes and perspectives are considered to be elements that shape the democratic cultural identity model, and that structure the interaction among its main features: political system, media and public opinion. In turn, according to Luhmann, public opinion is a structure formed by institutionalized issues conveyed by the media, but defined according to the political system's needs, that he calls *thematization*. This concept can be understood as a process of definition, establishment and recognition of major public themes throughout media action (Luhmann 2005: 30-32). Therefore, the author understands public opinion as a consequence of a selective activity by the media that gives relevance to a set of public issues. These themes don't intend to determine either opinion contents or decision or action; they serve, exclusively, to capture attention and to reduce uncertainty according to the political system's strategic decisions.

In Western cultural tradition of the public sphere, diversity and pluralism of voices, themes and perspectives are considered to be structuring democratic cultural values that society esteems. Furthermore, in spite of how differently it may be shaped in democratic politics, epitomized in Habermas and Luhmann's opposite archetypes, public opinion is considered to be the prime mover of democratic politic (Habermas 1984, Fraser 1991, 2007, Luhmann 1992, Schudson 1995), which, in turn, is framed by historical, political, cultural, and media development, as configuring elements of political communication culture (Hallin and Mancini 1996). The chapter departs form this acknowledgement to discuss the 'democraticity' of the Portuguese democratic culture. For that purpose mechanisms that lead to public opinion building will be analyzed, by studying one of its components, published opinion.

Objectives and Methodology

In several instances within the public sphere society debates public issues and public opinion is built through tensions, negotiations and consensus. Hence, mediation is a pivotal keyword concerning the structural and cultural identity of democratic regimes. Mediation works as a cultural-political tool for dealing with ongoing, dynamic, fluid, and conflicting processes involving several sets of actors in shaping public debate.

Within this process, pundits play a relevant role (Nimmo and Combs 1994, McNair 2003). Moreover, considering the ripple effect of the pundits' agenda when analyzing public issues. Hence, researching punditry offers relevant insights for understanding Portuguese democracy culture. Within this framework, the chapter will focus on Portuguese punditry and the analysis will be defined and conducted by the aim of discussing the 'democraticity' of the Portuguese democratic culture, which translates into a set of research questions that will be presented further on.

For that purpose four Portuguese mainstream newspapers were selected: daily *Diário de Notícias* (DN), *Público*, and weekly *Expresso* and *Visão*. These are the agenda-setters of several Portuguese public agendas, mainly in the political sphere and other media. Rather than wishing to emphasize the role of each newspaper, this research aims to uncover the general trends present in the mainstream press, as a constitutive element of public life in Portugal.[6]

The period of analysis of the study comprises the years from 2000 to 2005. This timeframe was established for the analysis because it corre-

---

[6] The research opted for analyzing the mainstream press punditry because, as previous studies have shown (Figueiras, 2005, 2008, 2011), other media pundits, i.e. television, radio, Internet, are traditionally recruited from the press. Since the 1980s the mainstream press is the place were pundits public credibility and prestige is built and confirmed. The symbolic status that pundits gain in the op-ed pages is an asset recognized by the other media that tend to recruit those already well-known public figures for their own op-ed spaces. One must bear in mind that this sector is rarely renovated, and that it feeds the logic of the *star-system*, characterized by always searching for and promoting the most recognized and the best media promoted columnists in the public's eye. The pundits who have such visibility are, generically, always the same, accumulating and circulating abundantly through the various commentary spaces: radio, press, digital publications, the blogosphere, and social networking sites. Therefore, in Portugal there is a strong tradition for pundits to be multimedia ones. Hence, by analyzing the mainstream press pundits, generalizations to the Portuguese punditry sphere can be made.

sponds to an historical period in the Portuguese democratic life when it is already possible to state that the Portuguese democratic regime, and within it Portuguese public debate culture, was normalized. Hence, within this timeframe it is possible to understand the Portuguese democratic culture at work in a stabilized context. Taking into account that regularity and continuity are main characteristics of op-ed pages a sample period was built considering January, May and September of each year analyzed, from 2000 to 2005.

The research will be developed within a two-step approach. Firstly, the profile of Portuguese pundits will be researched in order to identify the social fields from which pundits are recruited. A special attention will be given to pundits coming from the political field, namely their party affiliation. A professional biography was built to identify the pundits' profiles, considering the following categories (Mills 1981, Bottomore 1974): Academia (teaching, research); Culture (art related activities); Church (priests); Journalism (journalists); Media (media professionals); Military (army members); Politics (MPs, governments, militants); Liberal Professions /Upper Management (Public or Private institutions).

Considering the relevance the media have in contemporary politics (Meyer 2002), and the fact that the op-ed section is a place of social power that gives status to pundits, legitimacy to their opinions, and a leading role in public opinion building (Nimmo and Combs 1994, McNair 2003), what are the pundits' profiles? Will a diversified and heterogeneous profile to be found? And where are they being recruited? The research hypotheses are that (1) a high level of pundits is recruited in social fields of power, and that (2) a high presence of political pundits is to be found in the op-ed pages.

Secondly, in order to research a little deeper the 'democraticity' of the Portuguese democratic culture, pundits' agenda and the way they discuss national politics will be analyzed. The research starts by identifying pundits' agenda with a special interest in understanding the place political issues have in their agenda. The analysis of the opinion pieces proceeded as follows: first, the coder (the author of the paper), considering the sample period mentioned, provided a running account of the topics in each article for identifying the main themes that each op-ed piece conveyed. The result from this preliminary analysis allowed to reconstituting pundits' agenda.[7]

Considering Public sphere cultural matrix which understands it as a place where diversified themes should be discussed (Habermas 1984, Schudson 1995, Fraser 2007), on the one hand, and the relevance political issues have in news media agenda (Patterson, 2001), on the other hand, what are the dominant topics addressed by pundits? What is the relationship between the topics addressed in the op-ed pages and the news media agenda? What is the relevance of political issues in pundits' agenda? The research hypotheses are that (1) punditry agenda is mainly built by the news media agenda, and (2) that it is an agenda that revolves around political issues.

The results from the preliminary analysis of the pundits' agenda also allowed to identify the op-ed pieces related with the theme national politics[8] which constituted the corpus of analysis of this specific item of the research, making a total of 6870 opinion pieces analyzed.[9] To identify the way pundits discussed national politics, the study employed traditional quantitative content analysis techniques, and three variables were defined: Frame, Style and Tone, sub-divided into a set of indicators.

Frame proposes an interpretative orientation of how pundits debate national politics. Following the theme categories systemized by journalistic coverage patterns of politics, three indicators were built (Graber 2000, Patterson 2001, Siegelmann and Bullock 2000, Brants 2006): issue (public affairs substance); personalization/leadership (politicians' characteristics: professional experience, leadership abilities, character, competence, wisdom, physical appearance); strategy/horse race (tactic and political

---

[7] For thematic categorization an inventory of themes was built: National Politics; International Politics; European Union; Social Issues; Economy; Health; Education; Culture; Social Chronicle; Sports; Religion; Justice; Journalism; Terrorism; Others.

[8] For the National Politics theme an inventory of topics was built: Government affairs; Government; Democracy; Political Party; Parliament; Elections; Economy; Journalism; Scandals; Personality characteristics; European Union; President; State.

[9] For this research a database using SPSS (*Statistical Package for Social Sciences*) software was built for processing all the gathered information.

astuteness, polls); system/political culture (cultural characteristics that frame political practice).

Variable Style defines the structure of arguments throughout opinion articles, which means, the way pundits present their ideas, considering five modalities: analytic-interpretative/explicative (arguments presented in a pedagogical and complex fashion, intertwining context, causes, consequences); critical (questioning decisions or choices); apologetic (defense of a perspective, enhancing its positive items); irony (satirical and sarcastic writing) and critical/ironic (combination of both categories).

Tone allows an understanding of pundits' evaluation of issues, sub- -divided into six modalities: clearly negative, mainly negative, balanced, mainly positive and clearly positive.

Giving special attention to pundits coming from politics and journalism, the research also aims to identify how they argue national politics. Considering the op-ed pages cultural expectation of a place which complements information given by the news media (Habermas 1984, Nimmo and Combs 1994, McNair 2003), and where reflection, enlightening arguments, and informed discussions are offered to readers, is the debate happening in the op-ed pages reflexive-oriented (contextualized, informed, pedagogical, and balanced)? And how do journalists and politicians address national politics on their op-ed pages? The research hypotheses are that op-ed pages (1) tend to discuss political issues as contemporary journalism does (conflict-oriented, dramatized, and negative towards politics, Patterson, 2010); and that (2) pundits coming from politics and journalism replicate in the op-ed pages the logic of each one fields.

These empirical results will offer relevant insights for understanding Portuguese democracy culture, which will lead the research to its main purpose, i.e. discussing the 'democraticity' of the Portuguese democratic culture. Empirical results will be debated against democratic cultural understanding of public opinion, epitomized in Habermas and Luhmann's theory on the subject. Will public opinion's main cultural values, epitomized in Habermas' theory, be found in the Portuguese op-ed pages; or will its characteristics may be interpreted as empirical evidence of

Luhmann's perspective, serving the political system's self-referential closure? Considering pundits' dominant profile and the kind of mediation role pundits play and expected to be found, the research would argue that the Portuguese op-ed pagesindicate exclusionary practices contradicting ideals of inclusion and open debate that culturally defines the public sphere, thus reflecting Luhmann's theory.

The paper will proceed as follows: the first part will present a brief contextualization of Habermas and Luhmann's theory on public opinion – as both represent two opposite theoretical archetypes of democratic communicative culture – and it will also confront their thoughts with others in an effort to enlighten the discussion concerning the formation of public opinion; then, anchored in comprehensive empirical data, the profile of Portuguese pundits, their agenda and the way they discuss national politics, giving special attention to politicians and journalists, will be analyzed. The chapter will conclude by answering the questions that guided the research by framing its findings in the discussed theoretical framework.

Public Opinion and theoretical archetypes of democratic communicative culture

In western societies' cultural rhetoric, democracy structures itself around communication, and in this social organization model the public sphere occupies a central place (Habermas 1984, Fraser 1991, 2007, Schudson 1995). This conventional meaning underlies the normative understanding of public opinion that became a principle of legitimacy, whose moral and ethical character resides in publicity and in criticism (Habermas 1984, Cornu 1999, Garnham 2000, Keane 1991, McNair 2003). As Fraser states (2007: 7), 'the concept of the public sphere was developed not simply to understand communication flows, but to contribute a normative political theory of democracy. (...). Thus, it matters who participates and on what terms. In addition, a public sphere is conceived as a vehicle for marshaling public opinion as a political force.

Mobilizing the considered sense of civil society, publicity is supposed to hold officials accountable and to assure that the actions of the state express the will of the citizenry.' Therefore, rationality, and public debate became elements that have shaped the democratic cultural identity model and that structured interaction among its main features: political system, media and public opinion. In so doing, collective compromise started to be valued and built on an idea of proximity between representatives and the represented (Habermas 1984).

This democratic cultural understanding of public opinion that shaped European dominant intellectual tradition is epitomized in what could be called as the *habermasean* theses. For Habermas (1984), democracy structures itself around communication. In this social organization model the public sphere occupies a central place. Habermas (1984: 68) defines it as 'a symbolic place in mediating civil society and the state', and where citizens embody a powerful political role, through public opinion. According to Habermas, public opinion is considered to be civil society's court of reason, an understanding developed throughout the 18th century. 'In the bourgeois public sphere a developing political awareness started to arise, (...), and through that, civil society learned how to proclaim itself; meaning that public opinion started to be considered as the only legitimized source of laws' (Habermas 1984: 71).

Within this context, public opinion began to have deep political implications. Aiming for public good, society started to build public interest, through publicity and criticism. Publicity, understood as the act of becoming public, became a means to the process of enlightenment; in turn, criticism started to be considered as a pragmatic control mechanism for reaching the best argument during public discussions. In this context, autonomy, diversity and pluralism became public opinion's main cultural values (Habermas 1984: 84).

This conventional meaning became the normative understanding of public opinion that became a principle of legitimacy in democratic regimes (Habermas 1984, Cornu 1999, Garnham 2000, Keane 1991, McNair 2003). Moreover, Luhmann (1992: 66), considers that public opinion has been institutionalized as 'political society's «secret» sovereign and invisible authority. (...) And in this semantic shape public opinion has become the main idea of the political system.' However, considering public opinion in the way it was institutionalized during the rise of modern States in the 18th century generates, according to Luhmann, 'an incomprehension of the problem of the concept's inner complexity. What states and concrete operations, what physical and social systems are the sources of this opinion? If this question is raised, the concept's conventional meaning dissolves itself' (Luhmann 1992: 67).

According to the author's rationale, celerity and multiple possible combinations characterize modern societies, and that increments indetermination and social contingency. The growth in social differentiation adds improbability to articulation of interests between systems, increasing, therefore, the improbability of communication.

In this increasing social complexity, the author frames his problematic approach to communication within a thesis of improbability. For Luhmann (1992: 40), '...the main question is (...), how is it possible to establish an order that transforms the impossible into the possible and the improbable into the probable?'. In this sense, if on the one hand communication generates complexity, on the other it makes complexity reduction possible and allows the existence of systems. According to Luhmann, society grows out of an overcoming of impossibility, meaning that improbable, yet not impossible, communication can happen.

Communication, therefore, is perceived as a content selection process that obeys social systems' functional needs. For Luhmann, communication is the central operator of all systems, allowing their existence, operationality, survival and reflectivity (Luhmann 1992, 1998, 2005). Hence, in his perspective, if the 18th century public opinion concept were truly to be applied, it would increase social complexity and the improbability of communication even further. However, 'this doesn't necessarily mean that it should be abandoned, but that it needs to be reconstructed from a radical principle. (...). Only in this way it is possible to take political implications of the concept that is explicable only by its history...' (Luhmann 1992: 67).

Thus, Luhmann suggests a reconfigured concept of public opinion as a structure formed by institutionalized issues, obeying the media's relevance according to the political system's needs, that he calls *thematization*. Public opinion, as simplified communication, can be understood as a process of definition, establishment and recognition of major public themes throughout media action (Luhmann 2005: 30-32). Public opinion as a result of a *thematization* process allows communication among individuals, requiring their attention only for a limited number of themes. Therefore, public opinion is no longer a consequence of spontaneous discussion on public affairs by civil society in multiple instances, e.g. from television to social networking sites, but of a selective activity by the mainstream media that give relevance to a set of public communication issues. These themes don't intend to determine either opinion contents or decision or action; they serve, exclusively, to capture attention and to reduce uncertainty according to the political system's strategic decisions.

For Luhmann, the true meaning of *thematization* is to hide within its evidence what really can compromise the political system (1992: 85). In this way, public opinion becomes a sensor, a mirror (as Luhmnann puts it) that reflects political power and its other elements. For Luhmann, it is enough to observe the observers and that excuses the political system from observing the complex environment. In this way, public opinion is considered to be a helping instrument of selective contingency, as a social mechanism for reducing the increase in complexity (Saperas 1993: 91).

Hence, in Luhmann's framework, his disagreement with the 'rational--enlightenment' theories is well emphasized, as is the case in Habermas' thesis and in those inspired by it, which frames dominant European intellectual tradition (Luhmann 1992b, Frasier 2007). For Luhmann, Public opinion as the political system's 'guide-mechanism', its *'poissance invisible'* (1992: 83), determines neither political exercise nor opinion formation, but establishes the borders within which the political system is possible. It serves its own self-referential enclosure. Therefore, the political system's legitimacy depends on itself and relies on its own ability to survive, i.e. self-reproductively (*autopoiesis*).

In the democratic framework society debates public issues and public opinion is built through tensions, negotiations and consensus. Thus, mediation, i.e. 'any acts of intervening, conveying, or reconciling between different actors, collectives, or institutions' (Mazzoleni and Schultz 1999: 249), works as a cultural-political tool for dealing with ongoing, dynamic, fluid, and conflicting processes involving several sets of actors in shaping public debate in a cycle of endless mediation. The inherent tension in processes of mediation is a necessary condition for the debate to remain open and continually revised and re-constructed at each of its constitutive levels, which include production, representation, and reception of public debate. Jürgen Habermas and Niklas Luhmann perspectives embody opposite archetypes regarding public opinion mediation in democratic politics, and their perspectives were the guideline for the empirical analysis presented in the following section.

The Portuguese Press Punditry

Considering punditry as a place of mediation, an instance of reflexivity and of influence, and that opinion genre offers a narrative of and for public life the research regarding Portuguese punditry will follow a two-step approach. Firstly, the profile of Portuguese pundits will be researched; then, pundits' agenda and the way they discuss national politics will be analyzed. In the end, the results will be debated against Habermas and Luhmann's theories.

Pundits profile

Before analyzing what pundits argued about Portuguese politics it is relevant to acknowledge from which place in society they are coming from, and also understand their profile. Between 2000 and 2005, 249 pundits were found, divided into 80 coming from journalism and 169 from other social fields (table 1). Considering the 168 non-journalist pundits,[10] around 45% (N=75) have or have been involved in a political activity.

---

[10] Regarding one non-journalist pundit, no biographical records were found.

69

Table 1: Pundits profile (2000-2005)

Pundits	N	%
Journalists	80	32,12%
Non-Journalists	169	67.87%
Total	249	100%

The majority of these columnists has a vast and diverse political curriculum, carrying out top party positions and/or government positions, as well as other activities in other social fields of power, such as Academia, Liberal Professions, namely advocacy and upper-management positions (table 2).

Table 2: Profession of Non-Journalist Pundits

Profession	2000-2005
Culture	7
Politician	8
Politician/Culture	4
Professor	23
Professor/Culture	12
Professor/Politician	18
Professor/Politician/Upper Management	24
Professor/Upper Management	17
Upper Management/Liberal Professional	15
Upper Management/Politician	21
Media	5
Others	11

Considering party affiliation (table 3), the relationship between parliamentary representation and op-ed pages distribution stands out. Firstly, no pundit comes from a non-parliamentary represented party; secondly, the major parties have a highlighted position. The difference between pundits from the Socialist Party (PS) and Social Democratic Party (PSD), and the remaining parties stands out;[11] thirdly and consequently, bipolarization between power parties on op-ed pages can be observed.

---

[11] Bloco de Esquerda (BE) is an exception. This political party appeared in 1999, and since then has progressively increased its electoral turnouts. These results have a political explanation (electoral discontentment regarding parties of the left, and changing Portuguese values, especially among youth *in* Freire, Lobo & Magalhães, 2004). However, BE's communication strategy must not be minimized, especially its non-mainstream and provocative political communication language (verbal, scenic, and performance) and its ability to set the media's agenda. The disparity between the party's longevity, parliamentary representation (fifth force in Parliament) and its visibility is well exemplified by its over-representation in op-ed pages.

Table 3: Political Party Representation (2000-2005)

Party	BE	CDU	PS	PSD	CDS
Pundits	6	3	33	23	11

It seems that op-ed political representation is shaped by political parties, i.e. conventional representation (Freire, Lobo and Magalhães 2004), and is also governmentalized, not only by the prevalence of government parties, but also by a strong presence of elements accumulating opinion columns and public office positions, allowing them the power to decide and the power to comment on their own decisions.

These results confirm the research hypothesis. Regarding the pundits' profile it can be concluded that a high level of pundits is recruited in social fields of power. It is quite clear that pundits are originating from academia, politics and liberal professions. These elements, when combined with the professions of the columnists, reveal that the pundits' sphere, for the most part, is occupied by the elite Portuguese powers (Mills 1981). Thus, one is faced with a conjunction of individuals of elevated status and with both real and symbolic power in Portuguese society, whose presence in the op--ed pages can function in two ways: as a consequence of the status related to the social field of recruitment and as an example of reinforcing 'from the outside in'. It also represents the visibility and conferred status for an opinion column to positively tap into the career of the pundit and his or her originating social field (Bourdieu 1989, Wolton 1994, Luhmann 1995).

In which the presence of politicians in the op-ed pages is concerned, results also confirm the research hypothesis. There is a high presence of politicians in the op-ed pages. Regarding the political party representation, it may be possible to say that the news-value of balance is a criterion employed in the recruitment of political pundits, as the op-ed pages mimic the Portuguese parliament political configuration. Moreover, the over-whelming presence of politicians in detriment of a more diversified and heterogeneous composition of the Portuguese punditry undermines, therefore, its possibility of being an autonomous instance from the political sphere, and also of being a 'symbolic platform' (Wolton, 1995) for diversified social fields to participate in framing public debate.

Pundits' agenda and debate

Autonomy, diversity of topics and pluralism of opinions are relevant indicators of the democraticity of the public sphere (Habermas 1984, Schudson 1995, Fraser 2007). Hence, characterizing pundits' agenda and debate will allow one to identify the array of topics, perspectives addressed, and opinions argued in the op-ed pages, and thus adding elements to discuss the democraticity of the Portuguese democratic culture.

Regarding pundits' agenda, between 2000 and 2005, in the 6870 articles analyzed, a wide range of themes were debated, such as politics, economics, social issues, judicial issues, sports or religion. At first glance, this variety of subjects could indicate that diversity was guaranteed, but a closer look gives a different perspective.

Table 4: Pundits Agenda – main themes

Themes	N	%
Culture	543	7,90%
International Politics	672	9,78%
National Politics	3027	44,06%
Terrorism - 9/11	470	6,84%

Table 4 presents the main topics discussed by pundits and as the figures show, national politics was the dominant topic in 42% (N=3027) of the articles, followed by international politics in 10% (N=672) of the columns. The remaining 15 identified themes were dispersed among the other 48% of the published articles.

As results show, a short list of themes requires people's continuous attention. There are big thematical areas, like national and international politics, filled up with new and routine events that hold a permanent place in the media's agenda, in both news and comment format. Thus, and confirming the research hypothesis, it can be concluded that novelty is a central value for defining pundits' agenda, which revolves around political issues. By and large, pundits discuss topics that are at the top of the media's agenda, and they stop talking about those subjects when they lose novelty, which in contemporary media frenzies is rapidly. This tendency means also, that the op-ed pages have difficulty in being an autonomous instance oriented by its own timeframe.

The four main national political topics discussed by pundits (Table 5) represent 57% (N=3027) of the totality of topics on this issue. Concerning government affairs, elections, government and party politics, the majority of these articles were institutionally scoped, which is an angle that interests those related to political power.

Table 5: National Politics main topics (2000-2005)

Topics	N	%
Government Affairs	688	22,72%
Elections	498	16,45%
Government	300	9,91%
Party Politics	244	8,06%
Total	3027	100%

As already mentioned, journalists occupied a quota of 32% (N=80) in the universe of pundits and politicians represented 30% (N=75) of all punditry. Together, they dominated 62% of the op-ed pages. The remaining 38% were from Academia, Culture, the Church, Liberal professions and the media.

Journalists were also the pundits who most frequently discussed national politics in their columns (around 54% of all written articles on the subject), followed by politicians (23.5%), centralizing the debate on public affairs between both.

Journalists and National Politics:

Table 6: Framing			Table 7: Style			Table 8: Tone		
Indicators	N	%	Indicators	N	%	Indicators	N	%
Issue	141	12,62%	A-I/E	261	23,36%	CN	624	55,86%
P/L	75	6,71%	Critical	635	56,84%	MN	105	9,40%
S-HR	182	16,29%	Apologetic	81	7,25%	Balanced	171	15,30%
I-P/L	90	8,05%	Ironic	90	8,05%	MP	40	3,58%
I-HR	269	24,08%	C/I	48	4,29%	CP	132	11,81%
P/L-HR	103	9,22%	Not Valid	2	0,99	Neutral	40	3,58%
I-P/L-HR	231	20,68%	Total	1117	100%	Not Valid	5	0,99
S/PC	5	0,44%				Total	1117	100%
Not Valid	21	0,98						
Total	1117	100%						

Legend Table 6: P/L = Personalization/Leadership; S-HR = Strategy-Horse Race; I-P/L = Issue – Personalization/Leadership; I-HR = Issue-Horse Race; P/L-HR = Personalization/Leadership-Horse race; I-P/L-HR = Issue-Personalization/Leadership-Horse Race; S/PC = System/Political Culture. **Table 7:** A-I/E = Analytic--Interpretative/Explicative; C/I = Critical/Ironic. **Table 8:** CL = Clearly Negative; MN = Mainly Negative; MP = Mainly Positive; CP = Clearly Positive;

Considering tables 6 to 8, journalists' debate on national politics was mainly framed (table 6) as «issue/horse racing» (N=269, 24.08%); «critically» styled (table 7) (56.84%, N=635), and the prevalent tone (table 8) was «clearly negative» (55.86%, N=624). If tones were merged it would be possible to conclude that journalist's evaluation of national politics is really unfavorable (65.26%, N=729), leaving behind the more «balanced» and «neutral» (18.88%, N=211) tones, as well as the favorable ones (15.39%, N=172).

An opinion article published by Luís Delgado (journalist of DN) in January 10th, 2000, illustrates these tendencies by criticizing in a very negative tone the work of the then Minister for Public Works: 'João Cravinho's declarations can only be understood as a weak excuse for having done nothing during the four years that he's been in Government. There isn't a single work, a single decision that has remained in our memory.'

Strategy framing (tactical and political astuteness), critical style and the clearly negative tone that dominated journalists' opinion articles, is also well exemplified in José António Saraiva's (editor of *Expresso*) article on the Portuguese Prime-Minister at that time, António Guterres, on

May 12th 2001: 'When all were expecting something novel, a sentence, a different word, Guterres just repeated what everybody already knew. (...). By appearing in the political conference without anything to offer, Guterres not only disappointed everybody, but also didn't give delegates, guests or journalists a single reason to have gone there.'

Politicians and National Politics:

Table 9: Frame			Table 10: Style			Table 11: Tone		
Indicators	N	%	Indicators	N	%	Indicators	N	%
Issue	129	18,24%	A-I/E	257	36,35%	CN	370	52,33%
P/L	22	3,11%	Critical	298	42,15%	MN	46	6,50%
S-HR	55	7,77%	Apologetic	98	13,86%	Balanced	108	15,27%
I-P/L	96	13,57%	Ironic	30	4,24%	MP	22	3,11%
I-HR	227	32,10%	C/I	21	2,97%	CP	140	19,80%
P/L-HR	32	4,52%	Not Valid	3	0,99	Neutral	13	1,83%
I-P/L-HR	132	18,67%	Total	707	100%	Not Valid	8	0,98
S/PC	0	0,00%				Total	707	100%
Not Valid	14	0,98						
Total	707	100%						

Legend Table 9: P/L = Personalization/Leadership; S-HR = Strategy-Horse Race; I-P/L = Issue – Personalization/Leadership; I-HR = Issue-Horse Race; P/L-HR = Personalization/Leadership-Horse race; I-P/L-HR = Issue-Personalization/Leadership-Horse Race; S/PC = System/Political Culture. **Table 10:** A-I/E = Analytic--Interpretative/Explicative; C/I = Critical/Ironic. **Table 11:** CL = Clearly Negative; MN = Mainly Negative; MP = Mainly Positive; CP – Clearly Positive;

Tables 9 to 11 show how politicians discussed national politics in their columns. As the figures show, this topic is mainly framed (table 9) as «issue/strategy-horse race» (32.10%, N=227), followed by «issue» (18.24%, N=129); «critically» (42.15%, N=298) and «analytic-interpretative/explicative» (36.35%, N=257) styled (table 10). Considering the merging of tones (table 11), data show that unfavorable tones (58.83%, N=416) prevailed over favorable (22,91%, N=162) and balanced (15.27%, N=108) ones.

These results show two different positions regarding politicians. On the one hand, they write considering the substance of issues, in an analytical, balanced and favorable way; and, on the other, they write in a very critical, negative and distrustful fashion about national politics, just as journalists do.

The evaluation of how politicians commented on Portuguese politics during the period analyzed allows an understanding of the dual shades of their articles. More than evoking two different positions on op-ed pages, it reveals a differentiated strategic approach regarding the object of their commentary. The combative format makes use of accusations, unilateral explanations, presentation of motives and carefully chosen facts. It enhances protest, condemnation, and intransigent opposition in a fight over supporters; and the apologetic format is reserved for their own political interests and for spreading a positive spin over the subjects discussed (Torres,1988).

These tendencies can be illustrated by the following opinions, which are framed in tactical and political astuteness, critically styled, clearly negative toned, and institutionally scoped, and which take into account the political pundit's political color. Correia de Campos (an MP and Minister of Health in the former PS's Government in 2001-2002) wrote on the Government at the time, headed by Pedro Santana Lopes (from the PSD, and also former pundit in DN, 2001-2003), on October 8th, 2004 in *Público*: 'Force is the weapon of the weak. If it were strong, the government would govern, instead of being occupied with the weekly critiques of MRS[12] (...). None of this should happen in a State of law.'

The majority of the columnists use op-ed pages to attack their opponents and defend their political and party causes. Politicians' columns have a propagandistic function aiming to lead the public towards strategic directions, through combative or apologetic comments, of which the following are a very clear example.

Medeiros Ferreira (a PS MP, when the party was in power) wrote about the EU Portuguese presidency on January 4th 2000 in DN: '...the Portuguese term in office is remarkable. It serves as an example of the political importance of the rotating presidency. (...). This is amply visible in the programme presented by the Portuguese Government.' A week later, Vasco Graça Moura, a PSD European MP, also wrote about the EU Portuguese presidency, but from the leading opposition party's perspective, in January 12, 2000 in DN: '...the Government, besides the usual bla bla bla, hasn't a

---

[12] MRS stands for Marcelo Rebelo de Sousa. He is a very reputed Portuguese pundit, Academic, Jurist, and Politician (former leader of PSD, Minister, and MP).

single consistent idea to articulate the defense of our interests regarding the EU presidency (...). This Government isn't ready to exist in Europe.'

From these research results it can also be concluded that there were almost no figures framed as «system/political culture». This frame contextualizes subjects according to political and social values that frame Portuguese society, and the absence of this perspective reflects a scant civic pedagogic component in op-ed pages. Consequently, citizens' involvement in public affairs is scarcely present in pundits' articles. Adding to that the institutional scopes prevalent in op-ed pages, it can be concluded that shaping the debate around institutional politics circumscribes discussion within the political system and excludes citizens as a counterpart in public debate.

These findings stimulate also a reflection regarding the way journalists and politicians write about national politics, how they position themselves in the op-ed section, and symbolic benefits that they seem to get from it, particularly regarding each other.

Literature on the relationship between journalism and politics (Patterson 2001, McNair 2003, Brants 2006,Graber, McQuail and Norris 2008) offer insight into this reflection. Scholars state that journalistic coverage of the political system is mainly critical, negative and strategy-horse race oriented. In recent decades, this coverage pattern has been institutionalized as an aftermath of the political system's orientation towards the media. 'Media-shaped politics' (Meyer 2002) is ready to be publicized without editing; but to spin doctors' propagandistic strategy, journalists answer back by covering politics in a critical, negative and distrustful fashion.

This adversarial position, more than revealing political disagreement, aims to reflect journalistic autonomy (in what Luhmann would call a system differentiation move), whose identity matrix was built, roughly at the same time, as an authoritarian political opponent and as political watchdog and representative of public opinion(Keane 1991, Champagne 1998, Cornu 1999, Norris 2010). And as Pierre Bourdieu says (1989: 69): 'understanding a field's social genesis and grasping the creed of the specific need that sustains it, the language game that is played in it, the material and symbolic things at stake in it, is explaining (...) the acts of producers and the work they produce...'

From the empirical evidence of this research it can be concluded that journalists' opinion articles are similar to their political coverage, reflecting what could be called journalists' 'anti-political class culture'. Empirical data suggest also that politicians use op-ed pages to attack their opponents and defend their political and party causes. Hence, politicians seem to look at op-ed pages as an extension of Parliament and journalists as an extension of the newsroom, thus confirming the research hypothesis. Therefore, op-ed pages may be perceived as a place for power struggle between journalists and politicians, where their social legitimacy as *the* representative of public opinion, shaped by each one's own identity and their relationship, is at stake.

While politicians have a formal legitimacy, journalists have a self-proclaimed one, built on their ethical and deontological professional values that allow them, in the name of public opinion, to check the political system's conduct (Cornu 1999, Norris 2000). However, in spite of the fact that the political system maintains high formal legitimacy, it is increasingly being questioned, which puts it at risk as society's reference-system (Luhmann 1992). In turn, the media's socio-political relevance in contemporary societies is giving them increasing power for constructing reality (Bourdieu 1989; Luhmann 2005). Thus, in contemporary societies, journalists and politicians struggle over definitions of news, politicians' control of their image, political interpretation of polls, and, as this research indicates, they also struggle over public debate control. In this way, published opinion can be seen as a privileged place for struggle over meaning, as a strategy for power affirmation by politicians, but, as this research seems to attest, that may be extended to journalists as well.

Conclusion

This chapter aimed at researching mechanisms that lead to public opinion building, by studying one of its components, published opinion in Portugal. For that purpose, the profile of pundits, their agenda and the way they discuss public affairs were analyzed.

Furthermore, by researching punditry the chapter aimed to debate the 'democraticity' of the Portuguese democratic culture.

Despite the fact that in western cultural identity of the public sphere, diversity and pluralism of voices, themes and perspectives are considered to be structuring democratic cultural values that society esteems, the empirical results of this study indicate exclusionary practices contradicting ideals of inclusion and open debate. Thus, the article would argue that, instead of promoting and reinforcing democratic culture, epitomized in habermasean theses, punditry may be interpreted as empirical evidence of Luhmann's perspective on public opinion serving, preferentially, the political system's self-referential closure.

This statement may be materialized, firstly, by the high presence of pundits coming from politics. Secondly, by political pundits' profiles, namely the reduction of complexity by centralizing the debate in the two dominant Portuguese political parties, the PS and the PSD – which have alternate government hold –, allowing them to participate directly in constructing and structuring public attention around a limited set of big issues, while fragmented in a vast variety of topics requiring short-term attention span, as illustrated by pundits' agenda. And, thirdly, by the fact that politics was discussed from the political system's point of view, as sub-section concerning journalists and politicians writings have indicated.

At a first glance, journalists' opinion pieces, together with their political news coverage, seem to express a menace to the political system's symbolic survival. However, considering the terms in which discussion takes place in op-ed pages, journalistic menace to the political system may be more apparent than real.

Discontinuity, conflict, personalization, novelty and recurrence (Luhmann 2005: 57-68) are forms set on binary distinctions that, as findings suggest, structure polemics that feed op-ed pages. Adding to this, celerity by which themes continuously succeed them reinforces the idea of published opinion as thematic structure immerging in a political communication process that, instead of jeopardizing political system, serves its contingent interests. Temporal *rhythmization* gives continuity to the 'need for discontinuity' (Luhmann 1992: 79), meaning that op-ed pages may be characterized by their 'ability to aggregate and disaggregate the environment and to use that to primordially assure continuity of a specific type of communication' (Luhmann 1992: 75), neutralizing, therefore, any potential threat.

Hence, at the same time that public opinion – and in the case considered, published opinion as well – allows the political system to manage individuals' attention span, public opinion also functions as one of its most important sensors, whose observation substitutes direct observation of the complex environment – impossible by definition, according to Luhmann – in a mirror that reflects the political system components, simultaneously observed and observers that act in front of the mirror: 'other people, groups, political parties and versions of the same subject' (Luhmann 1992: 86), such as journalists and their opinion writings.

Overall, it seems to be possible to suggest that the Portuguese democratic culture promotes exclusionary practices contradicting ideals of inclusion and open debate. It may be argued that published opinion serves less to establish external contacts, than to allow self-observation and the necessary reflectivity to maintain the political system's self-referential closure.[13] Therefore, if in the traditional cultural identity of the public sphere, of which op-ed pages are one instance, diversity and pluralism of voices, themes and perspectives are considered to be structuring values that society esteems and that allow the building of enlightened public opinion; the empirical results discussed in this chapter, however, indicate that 'there is nothing that guarantees the possibility of achieving real agreements, but there is a public communication that supports itself in this fiction and that assures its continuity' (Luhmann1992: 73).

References

Bottomore, T. B. (1964) *Elites and Society*. London: Routledge.

Bourdieu, P. (1989) *O Poder Simbólico/Language and symbolic power*. Lisboa: Difel.

---

[13] Against the background of Luhmann's theory, it would be interesting to analyze the recent riots in Greece, and the 'M-15' movement in Spain, as countermove acts against the Southern European political system *modus operandi*, which are making citizens feel excluded from political debate and the decision making process.

Brants, K. (2006) 'The Good, the bad and thecynical political journalism under attack' in 2nd International Conference on journalism and democracy. Lisboa: CIMJ.

Champagne, P (1990) *Faire l'opinion/Opinion making*. Paris: Éditions de Minuit.

Cornu, D. (1999) *Jornalismo e Verdade/Journalism and truth*. Lisboa: Instituto Piaget.

Cunha, I. (2007) 'Fins de mandato de primeiros-ministros: Tendências de cobertura/*Prime-Ministers end of mandate: news coverage trends*' in I. Cunha (ed.) *Jornalismo e democracia/ Journalism and democracy*. Lisboa: Paulus.

Figueiras, R. (2005) *Os Comentadores e os Medi/ The Pundits and the Media*. Lisbon: Livros Horizonte Publishers.

Figueiras, R. (2009) *O Comentário Político e a Política do Comentário/The Political Pundits and the Politics of Punditry*. Lisbon: Paulus Publishers/Portugal-Brasil.

Figueiras, R. (2011) 'Press Pundits and Portuguese Society' in *Journalism: Theory, Practice, and Criticism*, vol. 12(3): 317-333.

Fraser, N. (1991) 'Rethinking the public sphere: A contribution to the critique of actually existing democracy'in C. Calhoun (ed.) *Habermas and the public sphere*. Cambridge: MIT Press.

Fraser, N. (2007) 'Transnationalizing the public sphere. On the legitimacy and efficacy of public opinion in a post-westphalian world' in *Theory, Culture & Society*, 4(4): 7–30.

Freire, A., Lobo, M.C. and Magalhães, P. (eds.) (2004) *Portugal a votos/Portugal voting*. Lisboa: ICS.

Garnham, N. (2000) *Emancipation, the media and modernity*, Oxford: Oxford University Press.

Graber, D., McQuail, D., Norris, P. (2008) *The Politics of News The News of Politics*, New

York: C Q. Press. Habermas, J. (1984) *Mudança estrutural da esfera pública/The structural transformation of the public sphere*. Rio de Janeiro: Tempo Brasileiro.

Hallin, D. and Mancini, P. (2004) *Comparing Media Systems: Three Models of Media and Politics*. Cambridge: Cambridge University Press.

Keane, J. (1991) *The Media and Democracy*. Cambridge: Polity Press.

Luhmann, N. (1992) *A improbabilidade da comunicação/The improbability of communication*. Lisboa: Vega.

Luhmann, N. (1994) An interview in *Theory, Culture & Society*, 11(2): 37–69.

Luhmann, N. (1995) *Poder/Power*. Barcelona: Editorial Anthropos.

Luhmann, N. (1998) *Observations on Modernity*. Stanford: Stanford University Press.

Luhmann, N. (2002) 'What is communication?' in W. Rasch (ed.) *Theories of distinction: Redescribing the descriptions of modernity*, Stanford: Stanford University Press.

Luhmann, N. (2004) *Law as a Social System*. Oxford: Oxford University Press.

Luhmann, N. (2005) *A realidade dos meios de comunicação/The reality of the mass media*. São Paulo: Paulus.

McNair, B. (2003) *An introduction to political communication*. London: Routledge.

Nimmo, D. and Combs, J. E. (1992) *The political pundits*. New York: Praeger.

Norris, P (ed.) (2010) *Public Sentinel: News Media & Governance Reform*. Washington DC: The World Bank.

Patterson, T. (2001) 'Are news media effective political actors?' in *Political Communication*, 14(4): 445-455.

Saperas, E. (1993) *Os efeitos cognitivos da comunicação de massas/Mass communication cognitive effects*. Porto: Asa.

Sartori, G. (2000) *Homo videns.Televisão e pós-pensamento/Homo videns. Television and post-thought*. Lisboa: Terramar.

Schudson, M. (1995) 'A esfera pública e os seus problemas. Reintroduzir a questão do estado'/*Public sphere and its problems: Bringing the State (back)* in *Comunicação e Linguagens*, 21/22: 149-166.

Siegelmann, L. and Bullock, D. (1991) 'Candidates, issues horse races, and hoopla: presidential campaign coverage, 1888-1988' in *American Politics Research*, 19(1): 5-32.

Wright Mills, C. (1956) *The Power Elite*. Oxford: Oxford Press.

CHAPTER 4
BETTER OR MORE INVOLVED IN POLITICS?
THE INVOLVEMENT OF PORTUGUESE VOTERS IN
PARLIAMENTARY ELECTIONS

Paula do Espírito Santo

Introductory note

The voters' relationship to politics is a classical issue in Political Studies and has undergone important developments on a broad and comparative scale. The citizen's relationship with politics and with the political system have given rise to important concepts such as social capital (Fukuyama 2000, Putnam 1993, 2000), which is a specific reflection of social and political involvement and participation. When analysing the citizen's relationship with politics and with the political system, we should consider political and civic culture concepts. With regard to this topic, we have seen a great deal of contributions beginning with Gabriel Almond's pioneering article, 'Comparative Political Systems', which introduced the concept of political culture in the *Journal of Politics*, in 1956. However, the idea of political and civic culture has existed and has been expressed for some time, although not necessarily being mentioned by name (Tocqueville, Mead, Benedict) and it is an important conceptual instrument in relation to the individual's relationship with politics and culture. With further reference to this relationship, several contributions have analysed the consequences of political participation from the civil

DOI: http://dx.doi.org/10.14195/978-989-26-0917-1_4

community, in terms of the regular citizen's needs of adjusting to how the system is organized and how it is constructed by the State (Fukuyama 1992, Linklater 1998, Lloyd and Thomas 1998, Beck 1998, Klingemann, Fuchs and Zielonka 2006, Inglehart, Haerpfer, Bernhagen and Welzel 2009, Lavareda and Telles 2011).

The focus on how, in democratic systems, people can effectively utilise the system's political answers to their real needs and motives demonstrates a standing process of both adjustment and search, which represents a, permanently, unfolding path to that needs to be followed. However, In 'The Role of Ordinary people in Democratization', Welzel and Inglehart stress that 'the development of effective democracy' reflects the acquisition of resources and values by ordinary people that enable them to pressure the elite, effectively. The importance of this process, known as 'human empowerment' is generally underestimated' Welzel and Inglehart (2008: 126). In other words, the human potential that each Nation contains the basic skills for a better democratic system. 'Democracy can be effective only if power is vested in the people', considering a 'human-empowerment scenario that consists of three elements: action resources, self-expression values and democratic institutions' (Wetzel and Inglehart 2008: 129). These three elements allow a political balance between the powerful elite and the will of the people which can operate at different levels, in relation to each Nation's journey towards an improved Democracy. The most challenging feature of the process of democratization is that it is a major political challenge with what is, probably, a never ending out-come. However, the human capital strength obtained will be greater at each moment in History. As stated by Wetzel and Inglehart (2008: 136) 'the major effect of modernization is not that it makes democracy more acceptable to elites, but that it increases ordinary people's capabilities and willingness to struggle for democratic institutions'.

The importance of political participation is an essential facet of the way the political system, and the citizens in particular, understand and interpret their role as active members of within the State's construction. In a period of time where there is a growing disappointment with the direction that politics and of the economy has taken it appears that there is an active repositioning of the relationship between citizens and the political system. In other words, being politically active usually means being less committed to the electoral offer. However, it also means finding and building more demanding links to the political system while searching for more information, the sharing of opinions and a more critical and informed way of living politically. The global and generational growth of education has allowed citizens to reach a political moment in which they are better trained at school and in academic terms and are, therefore, each time more and more critical and knowledgeable about what they want, about politics and about politicians.

Remarks relating to the Political system and methodological aspects

The Portuguese political system is considered to be of a semi-presidential type. This generally means that there are two basic political ruling institutions of the State and Nation, which are Parliament and the President. In the Portuguese system both Parliament and the President are the principal political institutions of representation. The President is the main political symbol of the Nation, in both internal and international terms, as well as performing the role of supreme political and institutional regulator. The Portuguese political system does have Parliamentary elections every four years and Presidential elections every five years (limited to two consecutive mandates). The President, the Prime-Minister, the President of Parliament, and the Courts are, though, sovereign institutions, in relation to the Portuguese political system.

We considered a three election period, those elections having occurred in 2002, 2005 and 2009[14]. In 2002 the Prime Minister António Guterres

---

[14] The Portuguese legislative elections, which occurred in 2002 and 2005, were both important and unique. These elections were important due to their inherent nature during a semi-presidential regime. They were also unique for having occurred as a result of singular reasons deriving more from a set of circumstances which had dictated the end of the previous legislature than from the normal and formal reasons that allow for Parliamentary elections to take place every four years.

resigned due to significant losses in local elections. In the following 2005 elections, the mandatory four year term of office had not been completed because of the dissolution of Parliament. This took place during Pedro Santana Lopes' short term of office as Prime-Minster. Santana Lopes had been appointed after the resignation of the previous incumbent José Manuel Durão Barroso who, after tendering his resignation, was then elected as President of the European Commission.

Methodologically, this study is based upon three post-electoral polls, applied to the urban area around the Portuguese capital, Lisbon. This regional council is known as the 'Greater Lisbon area' and includes the eight councils around Lisbon[15]. The area in question has over 1.5 million voters[16] from a national electorate of about 9.5 million. This area of this study consists of all of the individuals who are included as voters in the resident electoral register. For each poll the most recently updated data from that year has been used. The electoral register is annually updated by DGAI[17]. The data for the three opinion polls was gathered about one month after the Parliamentary elections had taken place.[18]

The design and implementation of the sampling plan was undertaken in three stages. For the first stage a probabilistic based sampling plan of 600 individual voters was used for each poll. Each council was separated into its political-administrative divisions, according to the number of voters.[19] At the second 'data collection' stage the random route itinerary technique was applied, which implies contacting the voters at home,

---

[15] The eight councils considered are: Amadora, Cascais, Lisboa, Loures, Odivelas, Oeiras, Sintra and Vila Franca de Xira.

[16] In 2002, the electorate consisted of 1,559,986 individuals, according to the current electoral census. In 2005 the electorate consisted of 1,679,706 voters and in 2009: 1590669. Data from STAPE (Secretariado Técnico para os Assuntos do Processo Eleitoral) and DGAI (Direcção geral da Administração Interna).

[17] DGAI (Direcção geral da Administração Interna).

[18] The elections were held on the 17th March 2002, the 20th February 2005 and the 27th September 2009, respectively.

[19] This sampling division was made according to the criteria segmentation of the 'freguesias division (small political administrative divisions similar to borough councils in the UK), related to Law number 169/99, of 18th September and No 8/93, 5th March.

and following specific itinerary rules. At the third stage the method used was selecting one individual per home, this is in accordance with quota method sampling, where a segmentation of sex and age, based on the last 2001 population census is the recognized procedure. If we consider a poll on a scale of 600 samples, the sampling error would be ± 4%, for a 95% level of confidence, and is considered to be a strictly probabilistic sampling plan.

The data analysis was subject to a principal set of procedures, based upon descriptive statistic analysis. We also used qui-square tests applied on crosstabs applications. Although most of the variables were already tested in other studies, the questionnaire was internally monitored, before being applied, in terms of field work. Several test experiments were also used in order to acquire a better adjustment to Portuguese culture and to reach a suitable level of understanding for the average member of the population.[20]

The hypothesis we constructed is that, when considering Lisbon, which is the principal political Portuguese urban area, in conjunction with the election period from 2002 to 2009, the voters in question tend to be participative, whether in political or electoral terms. Furthermore, our primary question is: 'can we find an evolutionary pattern in political and electoral terms?' As a result, we believe it is both relevant and intriguing since Lisbon is the main political centre for a country of such small dimension as Portugal. According to results obtained from other research that has been undertaken, with comparable data (Cayrol 1989, Inglehart and Andeweg 1993, Boy and Mayer 1997a, Jaffré and Chice 1997, Norris 2001, Welzel and Inglehart 2008, Inglehart, Haerpfer, Bernhagen and Welzel 2009), it may be assumed that within the methodological characteristics of the study, Portuguese voters tend to demonstrate a participative pattern towards politics and elections.

---

[20] The interview' teams were made up of university students, from the Communication Studies' course, of ISCSP (Instituto Superior de Ciências Sociais e Políticas)/UTL (Universidade Técnica de Lisboa), from the 2001/2002 and 2004/2005 and 2009/2010 courses.

Political involvement and voting perceptions: results

The political involvement and voting perceptions section refers to a set of variables that seek to describe the political and electoral participation of voters, as well as their perceptions on electoral choice. When referring to 'voters involvement' we mean that which defines the individual's relationship with politics, in political terms, whether it be on an electoral, social or cultural basis. In the present study we take into question a short and consecutive election period, more exactly an evolving three election period (2002, 2005 and 2009). Within this research, the aim is to analyse the importance of various motives, especially the role of the media as a serious constraint and socialization agent on voters' involvement, and also to investigate the role of primary groups and political parties, as examples of relevant aspects that may explain the individuals' relationship to politics. In relation to this matter, we specifically considered five variables which are namely: attitudes and voting behavior; associations of belonging; situations in which the voters participated during the political campaign period; the factors that most influenced the interviewees in their choice of vote; and, finally, the moment when deciding to cast a vote.

In respect of attitudes and voting behavior, relating to the three Parliamentary elections of 2002 2005 and 2009, the majority of voters stated that they were party supporters and that they had voted in the elections. There was a proportional increase in this group in 2005, of approximately 11%, according to the post-electoral polls considered (2002: 52%; 2005: 63%; 2009: 47%). This rise and fall of interest in parties indicates a conjuncture phenomenon demonstrating an enthusiasm in 2005 related to José Socrates' own political enthusiasm and personality (table 1). It also appears important to stress the approximately 5% of individuals who said that they were party members. This amount remained stable over the three election period. This value is slightly above the average value for the individual party members in Portugal. These values can be explained because we are taking into account the largest Portuguese urban area.

From these values we should also underline the number of individuals who said that despite not being party supporters they had still voted in elections. This proportion is similar in the first two polls (around 20%) -

2002 and 2005 - and then rose (27%) - 2009 - which may be interpreted as a tendency to politically walk away from the parties. It means that a move towards politically 'independent' positions is a tendency that is eventually seen. This set of individuals is the most malleable and is more susceptible to influence by electoral campaign actions and, furthermore, is attracted to political-party alternatives. In relation to individuals who are not party supporters and who do not vote in elections, there was evidence of a slight decline between the three post-electoral polls from around 15% to about 6% and then an increase back to about 15%. This fall and rise indicates that the group of individuals who, usually, show possible indifference or feelings of rejection to parties and elections may include a significant proportion of politically interested 'converts'. The rise in the percentage of individuals' political and electoral interest which emerged during the 2005 election may be interpreted as high, due to conjuncture reasons. Reasons related to the less popular leadership of Pedro Santana Lopes, who became Prime Minister, after José Manuel Durão Barroso had accepted the post of President of the European Commission, in 2004. Santana Lopes´ mandate as Prime Minister lasted less than a year, ending with the dissolution of Parliament by Jorge Sampaio, the President at that time.

Table 1 – Relationship to politics and parties

		2002		2005		2009	
		Frequency	Valid percentage	Frequency	Valid percentage	Frequency	Valid percentage
Relation to politics	Is a party member	29	4,8	29	4,8	32	5,3
	Is a party supporter and votes in elections	312	52,0	379	63,2	284	47,3
	Is a party supporter but does not vote in elections	45	7,5	37	6,2	35	5,8
	Is not a party supporter but votes in elections	125	20,8	116	19,3	162	27,0
Total	Is not a party supporter and does not vote in elections	89	14,8	39	6,5	87	14,5
		600	100,0	600	100,0	600	100,0

The collaboration through membership to associations over the last twelve months is a topic that merits analysing the importance of entering into social participation and its possibilities, as a consequence of an associative phenomenon. The importance of associations in civil society is a traditional object in Political Science and Sociology (Tocqueville, 1835-1840; Roskin *et al.* 1974, 2003, Almond and Verba 1980, Bacalhau 1991, Putnam 1993, Putnam 2000, Webb, Farrell and Holliday 2002, Whiteley 2008). In Portugal, there is no deep tradition of associationism. The research regarding this subject in Portugal does not afford long-term comparable data. According to one of the first polls used in relation to this issue, the percentage of people who have not joined any associations was about 86% in 1978, about 84% in 1984 and about 83% in 1993 (Bacalhau 1994). This proportion may be deemed high, if we consider the wide range of available civil associations. According to present surveys, which relate to the 'Greater Lisbon area councils, in 2002 the range of individuals who had not become members of an association during the last 12 months was about 67%. This proportion increased to about 75%, in 2005 and fell to 70% in 2009. We may consider this to be a significant percentage of people. Those who say that they had not joined any association during the last 12 months were resident in the Lisbon urban area, which is the area offering more facilities and more opportunities for organization and mobilization in association terms.

If we consider those individuals who enrolled in an association over the last 12 months, the highest numbers are attracted to sports, recreation, neighbourhood associations, political parties and church associations. This happened in 2002, 2005 and 2009, despite some slight differences. We should stress that political parties and socio-political associations have a constant and also significant uptake (about 7%). In relation to this we should consider that political parties in Portugal, and especially in Lisbon, seem to have a mobilizing influence, particularly important in regard to sports or recreational associations. Consequently, we should also take into consideration that parties do play a leading and important role in sensitizing society to political and civic causes. In other words, parties still matter and are actively ahead in civil society association activities.

Table 2 – Joining into associations during the last twelve months

		2002		2005		2009	
		Frequency	Valid per-centage	Frequency	Valid per-centage	Frequency	Valid per-centage
Association	Recreative association	32	6,3%	24	4,0	24	4,2
	Sports association	40	7,8%	32	5,4	34	5,9
	Neighborhood association	18	3,5%	26	4,4	39	6,8
	Trade unions	13	2,5%	5	,8	19	3,3
	Professional association	12	2,3%	14	2,3	17	3,0
	Church group or association	19	3,7%	29	4,9	30	5,2
	Cultural association	13	2,5%	24	4,0	18	3,1
	Students association	17	3,3%	13	2,2	11	1,9
	Political party or socio-political association	34	6,7%	9	6,7	37	6,5
	Did not join an association	341	66,7%	448	75,0	402	70,2
Total		539		663		631	

NOTE: Multiple answer and filter question.

The variable 'situations in which you participated during the political campaign period' is also an important motive for analysis, with regard to the relationship that individuals have with politics. Despite the critical and influential critics of the early 90's about the effects of TV on democracy (Kellner, 1990, Popper and Condry 1993, Lecomte 1993), the social and political impact of TV remains effective. This is also true in spite of the fact that television is quite often not at all linear in the way it really impacts upon democracy (Noelle-Newman 1984, Inglehart Andeweg 1993, Huckfeldt and Sprague 1995, Page 1996, Ramonet 1999). The dramatic as well as the emotional weight of TV are eminent features that, according to Graber's experiments (1996) set up TV as a major source of political information, yet in spite of its massive scale and scope, this medium can reach a wider and extremely heterogeneous audience of citizens, including people with little or no interest in politics. The discussion on the consumption of information about politics stresses the connection between political, media consumption and civic engagement. In this regard, from a comparative perspective which includes several countries across Europe and also in the U.S., according to Pippa Norris (2000): 'those most exposed to the news media [...] consistently proved more knowledgeable, not less; more trusting towards government and the political system, not less; and more likely to participate in election campaigns, not less' (Norris 2000: 314). In most western democratic countries, looking at civic engagement is an exercise in discovering a set of constant inputs that reinforce and characterize the nature of the political system. The assimilation of such inputs by the political system and its civic structure, simultaneously, shows a very flexible system which is constantly adapting itself to the multiple circumstances of each political culture. Apart from the multiple inputs that are permanently generated by the system, there are those that are produced by the media, relating to different media types and consequently different patterns of political participation and trust. Comparative data across the E.U.27 reveals TV as being the principal medium of trust (63%), followed by newspapers (43%), radio (31%), the internet (22%), written magazines (8%)[21]. Some studies have already underlined the importance of the media during a public discussion of the ideas, which tends to have greater impact upon the newspaper readers and, specifically, upon those who have studied further education (Popkin 1991, Norris 2001, Inglehart and Pippa 2009). This tendency, however, shouldn't discourage the need for improving and providing more and better political information, specially, about those with less political competence. The experiments by Tilley and Wlezien (2008) indicate that additional knowledge can be of use to people with low levels of political information and sophistication, motivating a change in their political assessments in an expressive way.

From the various examples of this kind of political participation already mentioned, the most popular within this urban area included the categories of 'watching information on TV about the elections', as well as 'talking about the election with friends and relatives', followed by 'reading posters

---

[21] Source: European Commission (2009): *Special Eurobarometer 308. The Europeans in 2009*: http://ec.europa.eu/public_opinion/archives/ebs/ebs_308_en.pdf

and billboards about the elections.' Each of these three options were found at the top of the 'situations' most experienced, which indicate three different popular sources of participating politically, all of them with significant levels of interest and reflection about politics (and the elections particularly). Comparing to the first two ('watching information on TV about the elections', and 'talking about the election with friends and relatives'), the latter category ('reading posters and billboards about the elections') may be considered to be the most passive and less reactive. This data confirms the tendency that highlights the importance of television as a paramount support mechanism, with regard to political motives. This was also a conclusion that was reached by several surveys in Europe and across the world (Cayrol 1989, Inglehart and Andeweg 1993, Huber and Inglehart 1995, Norris 2001, Inglehart and Norris 2009). It also worth mentioning that about 10%, of individuals in 2002, 7%, in 2005 and about 13%, in 2009 did not experience any of the previously mentioned situations, which is evidence of a lack of interest not only in terms of civic participation but also in relation to the quest for becoming a better informed citizen. A note should be added about the internet and to justify its absence from the data analysed. The use of the internet for campaigning motives, during the nineties, was seen as a secondary resource, with small demand or even investment from politicians, and consequently with limited skills being employed (Lilleaker 2006). During the first decade of the 21st century, however, particularly during the latter years, the internet grew steadily around the world, and in Portugal, too.[22] However, in political terms, specifically during the 2009 elections[23] in Portugal, for example, the internet was not as widely exploited and used as it could have been. This is surprising when considering the investments made by the parties, which included inviting group of enterprises and internet specialists, working to promoting that medium (Canavilhas 2012). The limited exploitation of the internet's potential by the campaign sites, in Portugal, also discouraged the electors from using the internet as an attractive source of information, at least that is until this moment.

[22] From 2000 to 2009, in Portugal, it grew by 79% and to about 4 million users (Canavilhas, 2012 and www.internetworldstats.com).

[23] There were three elections in Portugal in 2009: Parliamentary, European and Local elections.

Table 3 - Situations in which you participated during the political
campaign period

		2002		2005		2009	
		Frequency	Valid per-centage	Frequency	Valid per-centage	Frequency	Valid per-centage
Situations	Talked about the election with friends and relatives	402	67,0	417	69,5	400	67,0
	Talked about the election with party members	113	18,8	140	23,3	124	20,8
	Attended a public meeting or a political party meeting	23	3,8	24	4,0	38	6,4
	Read information sent by the parties	152	25,3	211	35,2	176	29,5
	Read posters and billboards about the elections	307	51,2	338	56,3	256	42,9
	Read information in newspapers about the elections	211	35,2	223	37,2	165	27,6
	Watched information on TV about the elections	417	69,5	444	74,0	380	63,7
	Heard information on the radio about the elections	126	21,0	146	24,3	128	21,4
	Tried to convince someone to vote for a party	44	7,3	54	9,0	52	8,7
	Did not experience any of the above situations	62	10,3	42	7,0	79	13,2
Total		1857		2039		1798	

NOTE: Multiple answer question.

According to the present analysis, 'watching information on TV about
the elections' was an item that was important for groups with differing
educational backgrounds. This emphasizes, once again, the importance
of television as a means of support with a wide reaching social impact
in terms of its influence upon public opinion. In social terms, the importance of education is affected by profession, in this reading. Within

the category 'talked about the election with friends and relatives', the professions considered as extremely specialized and held in high esteem socio-professionally (for instance: Directors of Public Services and enterprises or liberal professionals), as well as the professions that tend to involve permanent social contact (for instance: administrative staff, sales people, shop assistants, door-keepers) showed a greater tendency to behave in such a manner. These two groups also included those people who tend to have read more information distributed by the parties, as well as those who saw information on posters, billboards, in the press, on television and on the radio. This behaviour, despite being reactive, shows an active and inquisitive attitude and, consequently, seems to indicate the development of an important political involvement in urban Portuguese civil society. This behaviour also reinforces the importance of the media as a key agent in the political socialization process, in an elective act.

Analysing the variables which focus upon factors that had the greatest influence on the interviewees' voting choices, reveals that television was the most frequently chosen category, followed by talking with friends and relatives and, to a lesser extent, newspapers, magazines and radio. These levels of choice are highly similar in both sets of data, in spite of there being a slight decrease of influence in all of these areas as 2009 approached. There is also evidence of a concomitant rise among those who considered that they had not been influenced by any means at all. These categories may not only indicate a conviction in terms of voting choices but also in terms of last minute choices, motivated by indecision. In the three surveys, there were a small proportion of individuals (from 5 to 7%) who considered that they had been influenced by polls, in terms of deciding how to cast their vote, which confirms both the importance of opinion poll research mechanisms and also of how public opinion is constructed. Newspapers, magazines and radio were the forms of media that were most selected as well as talking to friends and relatives.

Table 4 – Main voting choice influences

		2002		2005		2009	
		Frequency	Valid percentage	Frequency	Valid percentage	Frequency	Valid percentage
Influence	Radio	54	14,4	45	10,9	47	11,0
	Newspapers and magazines	91	24,2	66	16,0	89	20,8
	Television	230	61,2	225	54,6	254	59,5
	Talking to friends and relatives	115	30,6	101	24,5	108	25,3
	Party gatherings	8	2,1	3	,7	13	3,0
	Meetings	16	4,3	11	2,7	40	9,4
	Street propaganda	29	7,7	29	7,0	48	11,2
	Posters and billboards	16	4,3	19	4,6	46	10,8
	Polls	19	5,1	19	4,6	30	7,0
	None	75	19,9	103	25,0	79	18,5
	Do not know	6	1,6	3	,7	7	1,6
Total		659		714		761	

NOTE: Multiple answer and filter question.

It is important to reinforce the enormous importance of television as an essential mechanism when it comes to forming public opinion in terms of voting choices (table 4). This influence is reflected in news information about political campaigns and also in the debates promoted by television channels with party leaders.

The exchange and promotion of voting and political information between individuals, as part of primary social groups, for example between friends or family is conscientiously expressed, in individual terms, as an important means of persuasion. This reinforces the role of these groups both in relation to the political socialization procedure and also in terms of voting behaviour.

With regard to the moment of deciding which party to vote for (table 5), most individuals stated that they always knew which party they were going to choose (about 66%; 59% and 63% in 2002, 2005 and 2009 respectively). Only a residual amount of voters considered that they had hesitated until the last moment. This percentage of undecided voters increases when the number of people who had already decided how to cast their votes before the political campaign is added to the equation. The number of most undecided voters is, however, a little less than a quarter of the total, which is a significant value not only in terms of the necessary space for mobilizing voters but also for political democratic change. This mobilization of voters eventually creates the typical symptom of electoral volatility, for either better or worse, in democratic systems.

Table 5 – Moment of deciding upon which party to vote for

		2002		2005		2009	
		Frequency	Valid per-centage	Frequency	Valid percentage	Frequency	Valid per-centage
Moment of Decision Total	Always new on which party to vote for	278	65,7	291	59,3	290	62,9
	Made his/her choice before the political campaign	33	7,8	68	13,8	48	10,4
	Made his/her choice during the political campaign	52	12,3	74	15,1	71	15,4
	Hesitated until the last moment	60	14,2	58	11,8	52	11,3
		423	100,0	491	100,0	461	100,0

NOTE: Filter question.

From the three polls available we conclude that the people who have always known which party to vote for were older individuals. There were also a greater number of people who identified themselves as having taken that option, which reinforces the importance of consistency of choice for a party among the older generation. On the same note, there were younger voters (18-24 years old) who hesitated until the last moment when it came to casting their vote. We may draw conclusions about the importance of age in relation to the moment of deciding on how to vote, as was witnessed at both elections. This importance was confirmed, in statistical terms, by applying the qui-square test (0,0000).

The individuals with further education were those who hesitated the most up until the last moment regarding which party to vote for, as the polls demonstrated. Among those who always knew which party to vote for: the less educated they were the higher the tendency they had to behave in this way. This was a tendency revealed by the polls, in 2002, 2005 and 2009. Also the qui-square test confirmed it (0,000).

We may conclude that the moment of decision regarding voting choices is an important reason for pondering among youngsters as much as it is for more educated individuals. These two analytical lines may enhance the importance of voters' political competence relating to the moment of decision on how to vote. In terms of deciding upon party selection, there is a tendency for greater reflection about the voter's profile, based upon a search for information in the mass media as there also is through interpersonal contact.

Conclusion

The present analysis relates to the first decade of voter behaviour, within a compared perspective and allowed several aspects and traces concerning the characterization of voter involvement to be articulated. This was undertaken with reference to Greater Lisbon: the major Portuguese area for decisions on voting. The media, particularly television, and primary groups, which are key elements in political socialization, are both extremely important as they directly influence the voting selection process. In connection to this we have found that the relationship of individuals to politics also shows the major influence that the roles of political parties and associations, as agents for political mobilization, have. However, we discovered that most voters always knew which party to vote for (more than 65%), and that less than a quarter were more susceptible to the impact of several socialization agents.

Throughout this analysis, we have also concluded that the urban voting population in question is politically participative, specifically concerning

Parliamentary elections, even though participation in terms of joining associations is somewhat low. It should also be stressed that a larger percentage of individuals are party supporters and they do vote, and that this proportion increased slightly during the three elections time period being analysed. Watching election information on television was one of the most important factors that influenced voting decisions followed closely by talking to friends and relatives. This conclusion allies massive support, such as television, to reactive and reflexive behaviour, such as talking or discussing. This is a very positive and participative way of living and taking decisions about politics and, especially, about democratic systems. This tendency must be contextualised within the slight rise in proportion of those who (although still in a minority) took their decision on which party to vote for during, or at the last moment before, elections. This may be explained as not only being due to circumstantial reasons but also to reasons that may lie in the more comprehensive and reflectional attitudes voters have towards political decision making. Considering the data that has been collated, we are clearly able to confirm our original hypothesis which stated that when considering Greater Lisbon, the principal political Portuguese urban area, and in relation to the first decade of the XXI century, voters tended to be participative, whether in political or electoral terms.

The results achieved, although covering a short time period, demonstrate a sensible attitude from voters who have developed behaviour and a vision that is both electorally and politically participative, something that may be seen as a positive symptom in terms of electoral and political behaviour. This symptom may indicate that voters are politically participative and electorally receptive, whether in terms of paying attention to information about the electoral process or in terms of reflecting upon electoral issues.

References

Almond, G. and Verba, S. (1980) *The Civic Culture Revisited*. New York: Little-Brown & Company.

Bacalhau, M. (1994) *Atitudes, Opiniões e Comportamentos Políticos dos Portugueses: 1973-1993*. Lisboa: Edição Mário Bacalhau e Thomas Bruneau.

Beck, U. (1997) *The Reinvention of Politics, Democracy without Enemies*. Cambridge: Polity Press.

Boy, D and Mayer, N. (ed.) (1997) *L´Électeur a ses Raisons*. Paris: Presses de Sciences Po.

Canavilhas, J. (2012) 'E-Campanhas Eleitorais em Portugal: A Internet nas Europeias de 2009' in R. Figueiras (ed.*) Os Media e as Eleições: Europeias, Legislativas e Autárquicas de 2009*. Lisboa: Universidade Católica Portuguesa.

Cândido, A. (1998) *Condições Científicas do Direito de Sufrágio, Lista Múltipla e Voto Uninominal*. Coimbra: Coimbra Editora.

Cayrol, R. (1989) 'Le Rôle des Campagnes Électorales' in D. Gaxie (ed.) *Explication du Vote, Un Bilan des Études Électorales en France*. Paris: Presses de la Fondation Nationale des Sciences Politiques.

Espírito Santo, P. (2006) *Sociologia Política Eleitoral – Modelos e Explicações de Voto*. Lisboa: ISCSP.

European Commission (2009): Special Eurobarometer 308. The Europeans in 2009: http://ec.europa.eu/public_opinion/archives/ebs/ebs_308_en.pdf Acessed July 2013.

Fukuyama, F. (1992) *The End of History and the Last Man*. USA: Penguin Books.

Jaffré, Jérôme, J. C. (1997) 'Mobilité, Volatilité, Perplexité' in D. Boy and N. Mayer (ed.) *L´Électeur a ses Raisons*. Paris: Presses de Sciences Po.

Huckfeldt, R. and Sprague, J. (1995) *Citizens, Politics and Social Communication – Information and Influence in an Election Campaign*. New York: Cambridge University Press, 2003.

Inglehart, R.and Andeweg, R.B. (1993) 'Change in Dutch Political Culture: A Silent or a Silenced Revolution?', *West European Politics*, 16 (3): 345-361.

Inglehart, R. and Norris, P. (2009) *Cosmopolitan Communications: Cultural Diversity in a Globalized World*. New York: Cambridge University Press.

Inglehart, R., Haerpfer, C., Bernhagen, P. and Welzel, C. (2009) *Democratization*. Oxford: Oxford University Press.

Kellner, D. (1990) *Television and the Crisis of Democracy*. Boulder, CO, USA: Westview Press.

Lecomte, P. (1993) *Communication Télévision et Démocratie*. Paris: Presses Universitaires de Lyon.

Klingemann, .s-D., Fuchs, D. and Zielonka, J. (ed.) (2006) *Democracy and Political Culture in Eastern Europe*. New York: Routledge.

Lavareda, A. and Telles, H. (2011) *Como o Eleitor Escolhe seu Prefeito: Campanha e Voto nas Eleições Municipais*. São Paulo: FGV Editora.

Lilleaker, D. (2006) *Key Concepts in Political Communication*. London: Sage.

Linklater, A. (1998) *The Transformation of Political Community - Ethical Foundations of the Post-Westphalian Era*. Cambridge: Polity Press.

Lloyd, D. and Thomas, P. (1998) *Culture and the State*. G.B.: Routledge.

Noelle-Neumann, E. (1984), *The Spiral of Silence – Public Opinion – Our Social Skin*. Chicago and London: The University of Chicago Press, 1993.

Norri, P. (2001) *Digital Divide, Civic Engagement, Information Poverty, and Internet Worldwide*. USA: Cambridge University Press.

Norris, P. (2000), *A Virtuous Circle. Political Communication in Postindustrial Societies*. Cambridge: Cambridge University Press.

Page, B. I. (1996) *Who deliberates? Mass Media in Modern Society*. Chicago: Chicago University Press.

Popkin, S. L. (1991) *The Reasoning Voter – Communication and Persuasion in Presidential Campaigns*. Chicago: The University of Chicago Press.

Popper, K. R. and Condry, J. (1993) *La Télévision: Un Danger pour la Démocratie*. France: Anatolia Editions.

Putnam, R. D. (1993) *Making Democracy Work: Civic Traditions in Modern Italy*. USA: Princeton, Princeton University Press.

Putnam, R. D. (2000) *Bowling Alone – The Collapse and Revival of American Community*. New York: Touchstone Book.

Ramonet, I. (1999) *La Tyrannie de la Communication*. Paris: Gallimmard, 2001.

Roskin, M., Cord, R., Medeiros, J. and Jones, W. (1974, 2003) 'Political culture' in M.Roskin *et al.,Political Science – An Introduction*. USA: Prentice-Hall.

Tilley, J. and Christopher, W. (2008) 'Does Political Information Matter? An Experimental Test Relating to Party Positions in Europe', *Political Studies*, 56: 192-214.

Tocqueville, A. (1835-40/1973), *A Democracia na América*. Lisboa: Editorial Estúdios Cor.

Webb, P., Farrell, D. and Holliday, I. (eds.) (2002) *Political Parties in Advanced Industrial Democracies*. Oxford: Oxford University Press.

Welzel, C. and Inglehart, R. (2008) 'The Role of Ordinary people in Democratization', *Journal of Democracy*, 19: 126-40.

Whiteley, P. (2008) 'Where Have All the Members Gone? The Dynamics of Party Membership in Britain',*Parliamentary Affairs*. Oxford: Oxford University Press, 53(2): 328-346.

CHAPTER 5

TRUST IN LULA DA SILVA AND THE BRAZILIAN PRESIDENTIAL CAMPAIGNS

Helcimara de Souza Telles[24]

Introduction

In 2006, Lula da Silva was elected president of Brazil for his 2nd term with more than 60% of the valid votes in the second round. But his party (PT) only obtained 83 of the 513 seats of the Chamber of Deputies, which was very fragmented: 21 parties got representation at the national legislative. A decisive factor for the government to organize a parliamentary majority came from the fact that the president conquered a consensual popular leadership facing the public opinion. As a result, his main measures could not be directly contested by the political class, under the risk of punishment of this class by the voters. New presidential elections would take place in 2010 and not only trust in Lula was high (849%) but also 48% of the electorate rated his political action as excellent (grade 10).

[24] This article is a result of researches financed by the Fundação de Amparo a Pesquisa do Estado de Minas Gerais (Fapemig), by the Comissão Permanente de Pessoal Docente (Capes) and Fundação Carolina (Espanha), that provided me the necessary resources through the Projeto Pesquisador Mineiro (PPM) and the postdoctoral scholarship. I thank the Institute of Social, Political and Economic Researches - Instituto de Pesquisas Sociais, Políticas e Econômicas (IPESPE) for the given data on presidential elections.

DOI: http://dx.doi.org/10.14195/978-989-26-0917-1_5

The popularity of Lula has been a guiding factor for the rhetoric of his succession, as a strategy of clear opposition against the
popular former president would reduce the reelection chances for
the deputies and the election chances for the opposition candidate
for president.[25]

Chart 1: Trust in Lula da Silva – 1stRound, 2010

More   Trust   Less Trust   None Trust   NA/Nk

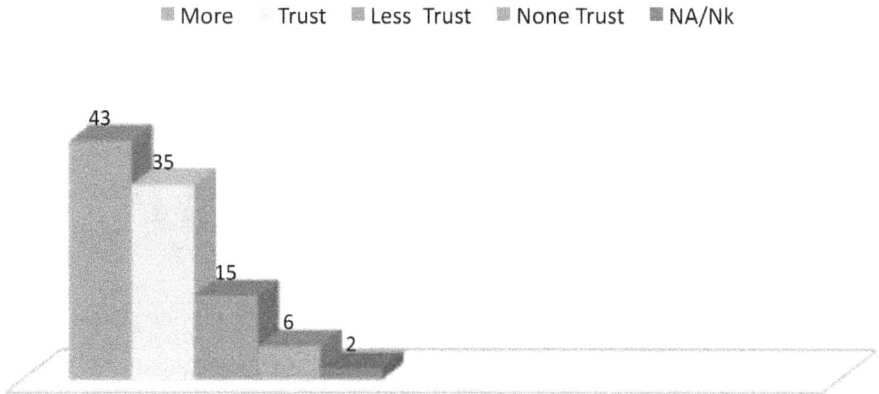

Source: National Survey on 2010 Presidential Election. Ipespe /
Research Group Public Opinion: Political Marketing and
Electoral Behaviour (UFMG).

It was from the statement of the electorates' trust in Lula that political parties organized their electoral alliances and adapted their political
communication. The campaigns would be axed around 'who would be
the best to represent the improvements headed by Lula.' The strategy
centered on a leadership only has an impact on societies where voters
tend to act independently of partisan orientations, which is the case for
most of the Brazilian electorate, half of which has no preference for any

---

[25] In Brazil, the elections for president and representatives take place at the same time.
The presidential elections occur in two rounds and the elections of representatives are
proportional elections with open lists.

of the parties and 7% of which even failed to answer which would be their preferred party.[26]

The Brazilian campaigns of 2010 for the succession of Lula da Silva, in 2010, evidenced the President and the continuity of the policies implemented by his government. Lula had already occupied this function for eight years (2003-2010) and was unable to be reelected, as the Brazilian Constitution does not allow more than two consecutive terms as Chief of the Executive. So he supported the then Minister Dilma Rousseff (PT) as his successor, elected in the second round with 56% of the valid votes. The victory of the *petista* resulted in the third consecutive national mandate of the same party, unprecedented in the political Brazilian history.

Voters evaluate the actions of the mandate and may reward those who made good governance and punish those who did not exercise a good one (Fiorina 1981, Key 1966). But elections are not only plebiscitary occasions in which the voter acts as rational judge of political and administrative actions. Besides the satisfaction with the administration, other theorists emphasize that the electoral preferences are a result of the individuals' position in social groups (Lazarsfeld 1948) and the psychological links between voters and parties (Converse 1964, Campbell 1960). In addition to such links, the context is also important because it affects the conclusions of the elections (Lewis-Beck *etal*2008).

For some theorists of the rational choice (Popkin 1981), the voter makes his choice based on imperfect and incomplete information. He makes use of cognitive shortcuts that give a meaning to these fragments so they become knowledge. The image is a cognitive shortcut that simplifies the decision and is either a typical heuristic vote or low information reasoning one. As information is crucial for decision making, to the extent that voters do not follow politics on a daily basis but need information to decide their vote, they can find this information in what is published by the media, the campaigns and their conversations

---

[26] National Survey on the 2010 presidential elections. Ipespe/ Research Group Public Opinion, Political Marketing and Electoral Behaviour (UFMG)

about politics. Thus, there is an interaction process between the daily collected information and the ones channeled by the media.[27] A large international bibliography agrees with the theoretical premises that '*electoral campaigns matter*' (Coma 2008, Beadoux *et al* 2007, Martinez 2004, Holbrook 1996), because they are able to bring large amount of information about parties and political conjuncture, build/destroy images and place candidates in the electoral race.

Political communication has become essential for the flow of information between politicians, the media and the voters. This importance comes from the fact that most of the occidental democracies go through a process of independence of voters towards political parties, which gives place to an audience democracy (Manin 1995). Citizens are less and less aligned with political parties, detached from those ideologies based on economic cleavages and exposed to various sources of information. The rarefaction of the faithful voter increases the electoral volatility and brings out new ways of voting - useful vote, opinion vote, protest vote among others, paving the way for the mediatization of the politics.

Various studies in Brazil have been focused on electoral behavior attempting to isolate the main structural and conjectural factors that influence the voting (Rennó and Cabello 2010, Martins Junior 2009, Zucco 2008, Carreirão 2002, Barreiras 2002, Singer 2000, Camargo 1999). These studies provided important contributions to the understanding of Lula's victory and his adversaries' in different elections. But they are still insufficient to explain the results obtained in 2010, an election in which the politician was not part of the dispute. For this reason, Telles and Ruiz (2010) tested a set of variables drawn by precedent studies to see what could have altered the choice of candidate in 2010. Through statistical analysis and multinomial[28]models, the tests suggested that support for

---

[27] Regarding the approach on media of the theoretical school of political behavior, see Mundim (2010)

[28] Variables used in the model: socio-demographic – gender – age, education, family income and region; political- parties, left-right scale, interesting policies, government, Retrospective: assessment of the economy; campaigns–exposure to HGPE (Free Electoral Advertisement Time).

Rousseff was greater the more positive was the index of trust in Lula, and otherwise when regarding Serra, (Brazilian Social Democratic Party--PSDB), who has been more associated with distrust in Lula.[29]Although Lula has not participated in the 2010 elections, trust in the president was the most significant factor for the voter's decision.

By observing the typical American voter, who has low involvement with political issues and little ability to develop coherent ideological thinking, Lewis-Beck *etal* (2008) argue that the voter is independent from parties and has little interest in politics. Such characteristics impact the competition, by reducing the ideological diversity of the supplies, by maximizing the use of the personal appeals and by increasing electoral volatility. In the presence of volatile and independent voters, the campaigns and political communication gain relevance in Brazil (Bezerra and Mundim 2011, Lavareda and Telles 2011, Lourençoand 2007, Oliveira and 2007, Ribeiro 2004). Advertisement displayed on the Free Electoral Advertisement Time can change the voting intentions (Figueiredo and Aldé 2010), both enabling and consolidating the previous disposals (Lourenço 2003) or as main source of information for the middle voter (Veiga 2001). Political parties are competing to obtain votes and for this reason, they have to influence the agenda and public opinion, and manage the image of the candidates. Campaigns consider the actions that are related to the disputes to establish public issues, with the objective to consolidate positions or change voters' opinions.

Within the analytical field that integrates short term factors to the electoral process, the pretentions of this article are the following: *What are the axes that guided the presidential elections of 2010? How did the trust in Lula impact these campaigns?* We assume the electoral market is regulated and that the characteristics of the party system affect the choices of the parties (Norris 2009). It is understood that the consequences of this position is that the campaigns are important for the

---

[29] Although it could be argued that trust in Lula is associated with the perception of the economy, the evaluation of government and economics only residually explain trust in the president.

vote decision, because they are able to *articulate the demand and the supply in a regulated electoral market*. To win the elections, the candidates make use of their functional and individual characteristics, such as competence, leadership and integrity (Stokes, 1963). Based on the Strokes' directional theory, the empirical answer found by this article is that *the axis of the 2010 campaigns was the dispute over the symbolic representation of Lula's third term*, as the former president could not compete for another mandate.

In a context where the majority of the voters are disconnected from the political parties, the personal political predispositions are *activated* by the candidates. Due to the high popularity of the incumbent, the competitors have chosen to adjust themselves to the demand and to make use of the only strategy that could increase their chances of victory: maintaining the *status quo*, personalist appeals and an association to the symbolic capital of Lula da Silva. Personalism is still highly present in Brazilian political parties (Baquero and Freitas 2011). There remains ahyper-valuation of the leaders,due tothe lack of trust in representative institutions (Moisés 2010). The persistenceof personalismcanbe demonstrated empirically by examining thedissociation ofthe voteobtained byLulain his previous participationsas a candidate for president-occasions in which he expanded his electoral base support -and the results obtainedby the PT in elections to the Chamber of Deputies. Since 2002, there is a gradual distance between the electoral territories of Lula and the ones of the PT (Soares and Terron 2008; Terron and Soares, 2010). The increase of Lula's support in the poorest classes of the population has been interpreted as the phenomenon of *Lulism* (Singer 2009). It could then be found, since the elections of 2006, a new kind of voter, more faithful to the president and less attached to the propositions of any political party.

The argument of this article is that Lula's leadership has been the main element to conquer voters. The aim is to check *how* the reputation has been important in the campaigns of 2010. The relevant question is not *whether* leaders matter or how much they are important, but *how* they matter and *why* they are important. The data analysis is based on two surveys, made with the Brazilian electorate in the two rounds of 2010, in September and October, they had gathered 3 000 (three thousands) interviews in each round, with error margins of 2.5 pp and a confidence interval of 95%. Beyond the quantitative survey, this article brings data from programs shown on the Free Electoral Advertisement Time, which is on radio and television from August on and during all the campaign.

The prestige of Lula in the public opinion

Nine candidates run for the presidential election of 2010, including Dilma Rousseff (PT), representing the government, who competed colligated with the Brazilian Democratic Movement Party (PMDB); José Serra, from the main opposition party (PSDB), who competed in alliance with the Democrats Party (DEM); and Marina Silva, former Minister of Lula's government and recently affiliated to the Green Party (PV). Considering their ideological composition, the coalitions could be formally classified, regarding the head and vice-president candidate, as center-left (PT/PMDB); center-right (PSDB/DEM) and center (PV).

Lula could not be a candidate for a third term, but he indicated a name for his succession: Dilma Rousseff. However, his candidate was running an election for the first time. For that reason, she did not dispose from an electorate already engaged behind her. Without any previous parliamentary action and being someone who never held major positions, the former minister inaugurated her first electoral experience under the sign of the dependence to the prestige of Lula.

Once the supplies have been defined, the campaigns oriented themselves around the president. The electorate prestige of Lula and the impact of his support can be seen in chart 2, in which we can remark that 64% of the voters could vote for a candidate under the influence of the former president: 43% would definitely vote for the candidate supported by Lula and 21% might vote for the candidate he indicated.

Chart 2: Prestige of Lula in 2010 elections: his support to the candidates

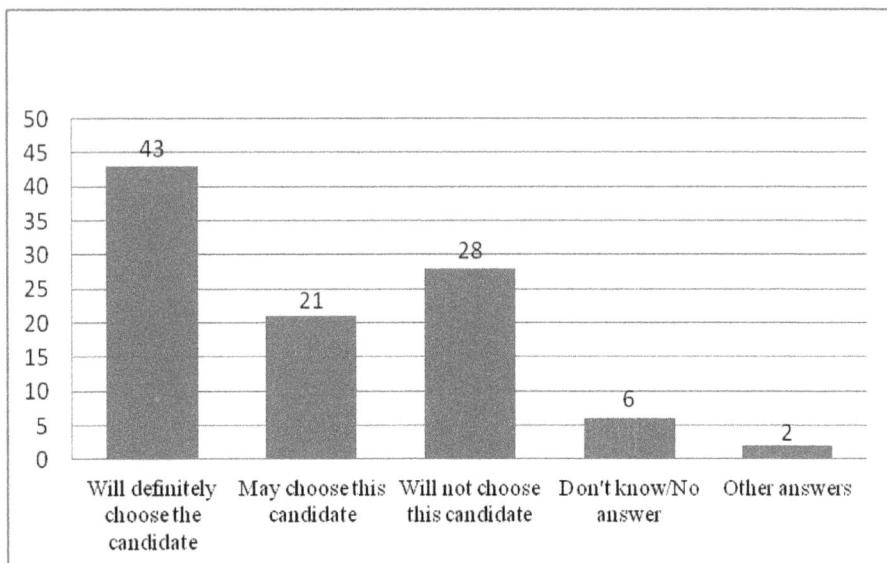

Source: National Survey on 2010Presidential Election. Ipespe / Research Group Public Opinion: Political Marketing and Electoral Behaviour (UFMG). Question: *Lula's support to a candidate of the presidential election of this year: a) you will choose this candidate b) you may choose this candidate or c) you will not vote for the candidate supported by President Lula.*

Leaders with positive evaluation are very important during electoral campaigns, and for that, Lula's support became the main element in 2010. Dilma's campaign so aimed to convince that, more than a substitute to Lula, she would make possible his own presence in the government. Lula being constitutionally prevented for running a new presidential election, the victory of Dilma symbolized the popular attribution of a third term to the PT, and the return of the former president.

But there were doubts about Dilma's capacity to politically and emotionally involve Lula's voters. Although a popular politician may transfer prestige, the degree of uncertainty in this situation was high because Lula had an emotional link with the Brazilian voter. It would be "easier to transfer prestige than emotional links" (Lavareda cit. in Costa and Marques 2009, s./p). For these reasons and uncertainties, even the opposition was trying to be accredited as inheritor of Lula's project.

However, the following tables show that Lula transferred his prestige to the candidates, and that this did not depend on the affiliation to political parties or ideologies. It is shown that Lula could alter election results. He became the main element of the campaign, surpassing the partisan identities.

Table 1: Candidate you would vote for if he was supported by Lula – 2nd round

Candidate	Frequency	%
Dilma	996	33,2
Serra	1472	49
Don't know/ No answer	536	17,8
Total	3004	100

Source: National Survey on 2010Presidential Election.. Ipespe / Research Group Public Opinion: Political Marketing and Electoral Behaviour (UFMG). Question: Finally, if Lula decided to support Serra in this election, for whom would you vote: Dilma or Serra?

The data shows if Lula supported Serra, he would get 49% of the votes of the electorate, meaning that Serra would be hypothetically elected, considering that his percentage of valid votes would reach more than 50%. And, as will be seen in the tables below, the endorsement of Lula would result in capturing voters. Lula could transfer his votes either to his candidate or even to his main opponent.

Due to Lula's capacity to attract the voters, the choice to employ the rhetoric of the situation and continuity was perceived as the only option for the competition. The candidates avoided placing themselves as clear opponents to Lula and, more than through their political programs, sought to seduce the electorate by emphasizing personal and functional attributes, avoiding attacks against President Lula but disqualifying his candidate, specifically through the social networks.

The Free Electoral Advertisement Time - FEAT: the messages

Political campaigns in Brazil are mainly promoted through the media. The advertising spots and the Free Electoral Advertisement Time (FEAT), on radio and television, are the most traditional ways of communication with the electorate. The FEAT distributes equal portions (one third) of the time among all parties; another proportion (two thirds) is allocated according to their legislative representation. The FEAT is displayed during 45 days, in two daily blocks of 30 minutes each. If no candidate obtains more than 50% of the votes in the first round, there is a second round and the time of each advertising block is shortened to 20 minutes. The frequency and time of appearance are the same for both candidates who succeeded the best scores in the first round.

The objective of the FEAT is to democratize the access of the parties to the media and to expand the political information, that can be transmitted simultaneously all across the country. However, the access to the FEAT is unequal. Parties with a small representation and that compete alone have only a little time of advertising. Major political parties or groups of parties get a larger allowance of free advertising time, resulting in easier access to their ideas by the public. Although the parties have access to display their political programs for free, financial costs to conquer voters are high. The professionalization of politics and the centrality acquired by television require the hiring of specialized technical teams, which led Brazil to be the country with one of the most expensive and professionalized election campaigns in the world (Rocha Neto, 2008). On many occasions, campaign expenses declared by parties in Brazil are higher than the spending of the American parties. The inequality occurs not only concerning the access to the FEAT, but as well the distribution of financial resources. Although the parties have resources coming from the party fund, the legislation allows donation by private entities. The money collected establishes differences in starting points and influences election results, which undermines the principle of equality among participants in the political dispute. Parties that are supported by richer groups collect more money and do campaigns that cost millions (Speck 2010a, 2010b). Moreover, there is a logic of concentration of financial resources: these are offered to parties and candidates with greater ability to interfere in the decisional process (Santos 2009).[30]

In Brazil, voters make use of the free electoral advertisement time to get information about the campaigns. Tables 7 and 8 present data that confirms the central importance of the media in the dispute of 2010. It can be seen that more than over the interaction with people or through the press, it was through the radio and the television that voters followed the campaign and the day-to-day politics.[31]

Table 2: Main sources of information on the campaign – 1st round –2010 Elections

Main Source of Information	Frequency	%
News on TV	1993	65,9
Advertisement on TV or Radio	581	19,2
Talking to people	116	3,8
Internet	97	3,2
Newpapers/Magazines	92	3,0
Radio news	43	1,4
Other source	10	0,3
Did not answer	30	1,0
Don't know	64	2,1
Total	3026	100

Source: National Survey on 2010Presidential Election. Ipespe / Research Group Public Opinion: Political Marketing and Electoral Behaviour (UFMG). Question: *Until now, how did you Sir (Madam) mostly obtain information about the campaign for president?*

---

[30] On the other hand, regarding the publicizing of information on campaign accountability: "Brazil has one of the most advanced mechanisms for collecting and publicizing information, with high access through the Internet. There is no other country in South America that has reached the same level. Only in the United States and Canada are similar systems found" (Speck, 2010a: s/p).

[31] For a discussion on theinformation, electoral advertisement timeandcampaignseeMaakarooun(2010).

For 85.1% of the voters, the television was the main source of information about the campaign, either to follow the political news (63.9%), or to watch the political advertisement (19.2%). More recently, social networks have gained importance in parties' strategies, despite the fact that only 3.2% of Brazilians have used the Internet as the main source to get information about politics. Finally, the usage of reading newspapers and magazines was not a characteristic of this public, as only 3% of voters acceded to the press to get information about the campaign. On the other hand, it is verified in Table 5 that more than half of the electorate (50.5%) stated they often followed the elections through the television.

Table 3: Frequency with which the voter followed the election on television
1st round - Elections 2010

	Frequency	% valid	% accumulated
Often	1528	50,5	50,5
Sometimes	859	28,4	78,9
Rarely	426	14,1	93,0
Never	208	6,9	99,8
Did not answer	2	0, 1	99,9
Don't know	3	0, 1	100,0
Total	3026	100,0	

Source: National Survey on 2010Presidential Election. Ipespe / Research Group Public Opinion: Political Marketing and Electoral Behaviour (UFMG). Question: *And could you tell me how often you Sir (Madam) are informed about the elections through: Newspapers and Magazines/TV/Radio/ Internet.*

The diffusion of the FEAT marks the beginning of the Brazilian campaigns and the prime time for politics, during which the voter is more attentive to politics. Although the main part of the voters who had already chosen their candidate claimed that they had decided their vote before the diffusion of election programs (63.9%), and more than 30% reported having decided their vote after the beginning of the electoral advertisement time. The FEAT was important to consolidate the faithful votes and capture the attention of undecided voters. Finally, more than half the electorate (54.4%) was exposed to the electoral programs in the first round of the 2010 presidential elections.

Table 4: Exposure of the voter to the Free Electoral Advertisement
Time (Radio/TV) -
1st round, Elections 2010

Exposure to the FEAT	Frequency	% valid
Yes	1646	54,4
No	1308	43,2
Did not answer	34	1,1
Don't know	38	1,3
Total	3026	100,0

Source: National Survey on 2010Presidential Election. Ipespe / Research Group
Public Opinion: Political Marketing and Electoral Behaviour (UFMG). Question:
Did you Sir (Madam) watch television or listen to the radio sometime during the
electoral advertisements for a party or presidential candidate, those programs
displayed on Tuesdays, Thursdays and Saturdays at 1 p.m. and 8:30 p.m.?

Given its importance as a source of information, the time available during the electoral advertising time is one of the main factors that orientate
negotiations between the parties. The time distribution of the FEAT for
the 2010 elections gave advantage to the candidate of the government.
Dilma Rousseff (PT) competed colligated with the PMDB, party with the
main representation at the Chamber of Deputies. This alliance allowed
her to dispose of the longest advertisement time, with 10 minutes and
38 seconds. In second position, José Serra (PSBD), colligated with the
Democrats Party (DEM), had 7 minutes and 20 seconds. Marina Silva (PV)
disposed only of 1 minute and 24 seconds, but still got nearly 20 million
votes (20% of the electorate).

The analyses of the FEAT allows us to check which were the major
"brands" used by candidates in their campaigns–biographical, disqualification, generalists, etc. besides the possibility to examine their speeches.
To analyze the campaign rhetoric, Figueiredo *et al* (2000) developed a
model based on the two axis 'situation' and 'opposition'. According to
this model, politicians hypothetically frame the world according to their
political position on this axis. Pro-government candidates claim that
'the current world is good and the future will be better'; the opposition
tries to convince the voter that the present situation is bad and could
be good in the future if he/she wins.

What has been the axis of the 2010 campaign? Unlike in the model developed by Figueiredo *et al*, the opposition did not take the statement that 'the actual world is going bad'. From the rhetorical situation – 'this world is good and the future will be better'- most of the campaigns to succeed Lula da Silva were limited to the defense of the *status quo*, lacking of candidates positioned as'opposition', personalistic rhetoric and some moral discourse.

But for what reason did the candidates give up the opposition rhetoric? Could good marketing change this tendency? In 2002, when Lula was elected for the first time, the candidate who represented the opposition to the then government of Fernando Henrique Cardoso (PSDB) had more chances to win. In 2010, the succession of Lula reversed this logic: at that moment, the tone was more about the representation of the continuity. The use of situation's rhetoric by candidates was due to the existence of a public opinion highly favorable to the president and that was mainly procured by the sense of well-being provided by economic growth and trust that the electorate had in him (Telles and Ruiz, 2011).

The political marketing, even if extraordinary, could not reverse the trend of continuity, which was strong and sharp. However, in cases where candidates behave as "similar products", a calculated marketing strategy and communication could make the difference. Thus, most campaigns opted to promote movement toward the center of the spectrum and political parties were discursively distributed into the same ideological space. The actions of the political communication were coordinated so that the main actor became President Lula da Silva. As a result, the agendas of the campaign were axed around the themes that would convince voters that their candidates were the best to manage the policies proposed by Lula. For competitors, the discourse was to maintain the *status quo*, without proposing significant changes that could afraid the *lulists*.

So, how to build the image of a candidate who had no parliamentary experience or charisma and was unknown to the public? Many are the discursive strategies that can be used during a campaign. Montero (1999) identifies thirteen of these strategies. Among them, the campaign of Rousseff widely used three of these discourses, always axed on President

Lula: (i) the invocation of the principle of authority, (ii) the search for consensus facing another authority orcontrol, and (iii) the image or icon to replace the word.

The observations of the programs shown in the election advertisement time brought us to the conclusion that Dilma performed as someone instructed by Lula to represent him in a third term. Being supported by the prestige of the former president, she would ensure the continuity of governmental actions for a better future for Brazil. From the discursive model of Montero (1999), we can observe that Lula has been quoted as an authority regarding his position as Head of Government. He was also a witness to the political and professional background of Dilma, who was accredited as a choice for the mission of representing him in the government. And to strengthen the connection of the candidate with the President, Lula appeared beside Dilma in all advertising programs. The main slogan of Dilma's programs – 'For Brazil to keep changing'-and numerous spots communicated her association with the President.

The experiment of 'transfer of prestige' can be illustrated by the program aired during the last FEAT[32] before the 1st round, which summed up the discursive strategy of this campaign. Lula speaks to Brazil as the greatest political authority in the country. Beyond an authority, the president is the witness and icon of the program. In this testimony, he unites the electorate by means of positive feelings of affection, stating that 'to vote for Dilma is to vote for me'. But he also appeals to fear, concluding with a threat, saying that 'with Dilma, nothing will stop':

Lula: You, who believe in me and my government: do not doubt us, vote for Dilma. Like me, Dilma cares about poor people, respects life, peace, freedom and religion. Voting for Dilma is voting for me, with the conviction of a better government. Brazil is on another level today, the government works hard and with Dilma, nothing will stop. She is the sure way to keep Brazil changing (ROUSSEFF, FEAT, 9/30/10).

---

[32] The FEAT was on air from August 17 to October 28 of 2010, with an interval between the 1st and 2nd rounds.

Serra (PSDB) adopted the slogan 'Brazil can do more'and opted for the speech that Montero (1999) identifies as 'depolitization', meaning the avoidance of conflicting content. He represents the main opposition to the government, representing a weak position where public opinion is satisfied with the current world. He was the wrong choice of candidate, completely misplaced – no marketing action could make Serra win if he employed the rhetoric of opposition. But a dubious speech could improve his position and get him to run the second round against Dilma Rousseff.

In 2010, Serra's campaign was ambiguous: he was neither situation nor opposition. He stated that the current world was good and he was the most appropriate choice to continue with the good things and improve what was bad. Serra fought for the *lulist* electorate and, in a questionable episode concerning effectiveness, used the image of President Lula for his own television program. Alongside Fernando Henrique Cardoso, former president from PSDB, Lula was shown as being responsible for the positive changes through which the country passed.

By analyzing all the programs shown during the first round, Panke *et al* (2011) found the prevalence of personalism and negative campaign on advertising, Serra's television program, aired in FEAT during the first round, dealt mainly with his biography, history and political accomplishments (50% as a candidate). A significant amount of time was devoted to the disqualification of the candidate Rousseff (14%). (Panke *et al*, 2011: 11).

Despite some mistakes during his campaign, Serra benefited from his exposure in the media. Bezerra and Mundim (2011) made an econometric model in which they included media variables and concluded that 'voters with more political attention- that capture precisely the exposure and the approval of voters to the flow of political information available, especially for the press coverage - were more likely to vote for Serra than for Rousseff.' Although the number of informed voters that are aware of politics is a minority in Brazil, among the few people most exposed to media coverage, the probability of voting for Serra was greater.

In 2010, the scenario of polarization between the PT and the PSDB, usual during the Brazilian presidential elections, was altered by the presence of Marina Silva (PV).[33] With only 1.23 minutes on TV, the candidate of the PV candidate obtained more than 19.6 million votes and generated a'green wave':

If there was something that could be appropriately called 'wave' in that election, it had been created by Marina at the end of the first round. Well, if throughout the whole campaign the curve of mentions to Dilma was typically placed higher than the others, the night before the first round Marina Silva's mentions on Twitter had already been at a similar level as Dilma's. (Silva *et al* 2011: 16)

Votes for this candidate were responsible for leading to a second round, which opposed Dilma Rousseff and Serra. Marina, a former minister of Lula's government, claimed that she had helped the President carry out good projects, but did not take responsibility for the mistakes made by that administration. She appeared as a new political force and a protector of the ethics that PT formerly represented, making the impression that the party had abandoned its ethical principles when it came to govern the country. She also introduced her life story and her background in poverty, similarly to Lula, and placed herself as the inheritor of the claims of the social movements.

Marina Silva invested in social networks and reached out to a young population connected to new technologies, performing an original campaign. Since she had little time in which to display her electoral program, she worked around her low visibility in traditional media by choosing to invest in *online* and *offline* networks. Marina tried to capture potential PT voters who were dissatisfied with the political problems and cases of corruption inside the government. But she also spoke to the middle class and to the most conservative religious groups, particularly the evangelicals, as could be testified in Belo Horizonte (Telles and Dias2011).

According to Panke *et al* (2011), the Green candidate devoted a significant part of her program to social issues. But she also used part of her time to

---

[33] In 2002, Ciro and Garotinh ogot more than 30% of the votes, but none of them could achieve individually the vote for Marina.

disqualify competitors, without directly attacking Lula, spared by all the main candidates. This strategy worked and Marina reached first place in important capitals and cities which had until then been islands of the government and administered by the PT, such as Belo Horizonte and Brasilia.

The electoral campaign was key for all candidates. It allowed Dilma to be associated to President Lula, and so to represent continuity; it allowed Serra to reduce his rejection, to penetrate into segments of the middle classes and to consolidate the opposition in the South and Center-west regions of the country. As for Marina Silva, the campaign allowed her to establish a connection with a portion of the public that felt dissatisfied with the country's political situation and made it possible for her to present her candidature as an alternative for change.

Voters and the image of the campaigns

The behaviour related to the act of voting cannot be explained only as an effect of the calculations made by party leaders. One has to wonder how the voter would react to political strategies and electoral engineering. The question of how votes are decided in a particular election is subject to how the voter expresses his circumstantial feelings towards parties, the conjectural problems and his position relatively to the instrumental and symbolic qualities of the candidates. When these elements lead the voter to the same direction, he will show interest in the campaign.The guidelines contained in the same direction consolidate previous preferences; contrary to pressures that can result in indifference toward the candidate (Converse 1964).

The success of former Minister Dilma assumed that voters should be predisposed to vote for the continuity of the PT government; at the same time, the candidate should be identified as the one having the best personal and functional attributes to represent this continuity. In the 2010 elections, in addition to these classical elements, the possibility of a transference of votes from President Lula to his candidate was the main factor to be considered. Empirically, the questions that would be asked were the following: What is the perception of the present and future world held by the electorate? How did they evaluate the government defended by the candidate? Are voters willing to maintain the current situation?

Chart 3: Voting intentions, 1st and 2nd round – 2010 Presidential

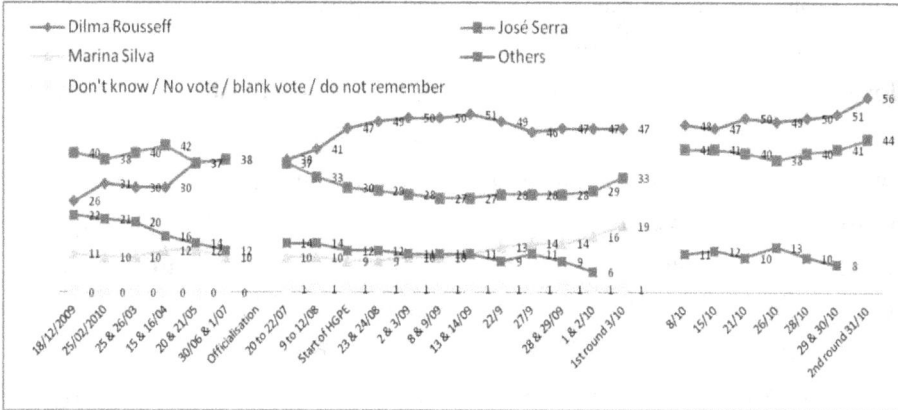

Source: Datafolha

In the opinion surveys, the curves of voting intentions show the continuous growth of the PT candidate, who surpassed her main opposition candidate, Serra (PSDB), while still in the pre-campaign period - before the start of the FEAT. The central matter was to clarify whether the support obtained by Dilma Rousseff in the pre-campaign period was *circumstantial* or *crystallized*. In July 2010, two variables indicated the wish to confirm the continuity: the satisfaction with governmental policies (76%) and the approbation of the methods used by Lula to administrate the country (83%). In addition to that, voters wanted a president who would give continuity to the current government, or made only a few changes (65%).[34] This consolidated the idea that the election should maintain the status quo and a predisposition to the use of retrospective vote - where voters examine the background of candidates/coalitions and estimate the possible effects of their permanence in the future. This combination of positive evaluations certainly advantaged the candidate of the government.

---

[34] IBOPE, JOB631/2010, April of 2010.

Another point concerns the voters informed by the partisan's preference. The party of the candidate had the sympathy of a considerable part of the electorate. Not less than 30% said they prefer the PT; that result reached 37% in the Northeast, but only 16% of the electorate in the South. The profile of *petism* has been changing and is growing within the layers of society with of lower income and education levels. Many voters remain loyal to the party, even when leaders do not bear attitudes consistent with their expectations. This can be explained by the presence of a mechanism of selective inattention in the cognitive map of voters; in other words, what individuals perceive about the party is affected by what they want to receive (Converse1964). In a competitive election, the fact that the candidate starts a campaign with many voters willing to choose their party makes a significant difference in the stability of their voting results.

Dilma Roussef needed the prestige of the president. For that reason, the pre-campaign focused on the image of Lula da Silva. The result was that, in July 2010, 80% of voters were already aware that the former minister was being supported by the president. However, this strategy could be insufficient: although one third of the electorate said they would vote for the candidate nominated by Lula, other 32% were willing to vote *depending on who is the candidate*[35]. This meant that on the one hand Lula transferred votes, but on the other hand, Dilma Rousseff would have to present herself to voters who were willing to follow the advice of the president, but who would also evaluate what she had to offer. The work to persuade those voters turned out to depend only on the candidate and, in this aspect, the political marketing would be crucial to project her image.

Another dimension interferes with the conduct of the voter: their orientation relatively to the candidate, their symbolic and instrumental qualities. Serra was regarded as the most experienced (64%), most fulfilling (40%) and most prepared to act as (45%). But his weakness was located in another cleavage: 45% believed that the candidate, if elected, would defend the rich and big business names (50%), and believed that he was the most authoritarian (35%). In the opposite direction, the strength of

---

[35] Instituto Vox Populi, 15th and 18th of May of 2010.

Dilma resided in an image associated with the defense of the poor (37%) and the women (45%).[36]

The candidates used the political marketing to reduce their weakest points. But campaigns are effective when they strenghten elements already available, as political guidelines act as filters for the reception of the information provided. It was up to political marketing to construct the image of Dilma beyond a faithfull follower of the candidate Lula da Silva, and Serra needed to establish his speech of change without losing his loyal voters, since the election was fought under the sign of continuity. Dilma achieved to be associated with important pillars as a strong economy.

Chart 5: Perception of the campaigns of Dilma and Serra by the electorate – 1°. Turno, 2010

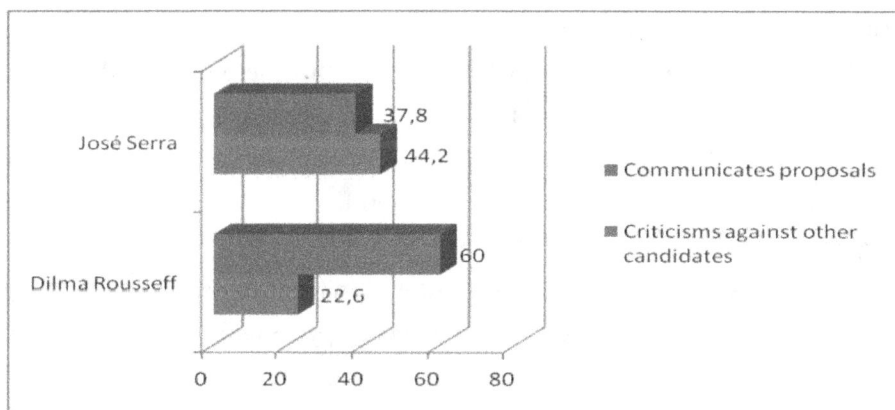

Source: National Survey on 2010 Presidential Election. Ipespe / Research Group Public Opinion: Political Marketing and Electoral Behaviour (UFMG). Question: *In your opinion, what does (READ THE NAME OF THE CANDIDATE) do the most during his/her campaign: communicates proposals, or criticizes other candidates? None of these (DO NOT READ) DN NA.*

As seen through the evolution of voting intentions, Dilma started the pre-campaign placed ahead Serra, but it was with the beginning of FEAT that the candidate consolidated her support, increasing the distance between

---

[36] Datafolha, 20th and 21st of May of 2010

her and the opponent. The electoral program was important for her to communicate positively with the voter and to be strongly associated to the best evaluated President of the history of Brazil. The campaign proposed by Serra was, on the contrary, perceived by voters as a campaign that was mainly criticizing the other candidates (44.2%) instead of communicating proposals (37.8%). Above all, despite articulating the rhetoric of continuity, Serra was perceived by voters as the anti-Lula, with 75% of the electorate indicating him as an opponent to the president.

Conclusion

In 2010, the voter was satisfied with the political performance of Lula, trusted him and did not want changes. This satisfaction would hardly be modified by political marketing, what indicated that the presidential election would be based on the choice of the candidate who would better represent the continuity. Despite the fact that voters become increasingly pragmatic in their choices, personalism is not something that can be forgotten in Brazilian politics.Lula's leadership was the main element mobilized in the 2010 elections. To captivate the *lulists*, the parties made use of the situation axe and the strategies reproduced the classic patterns of personalization, monopolizing rhetoric of continuity and moral judgments.

These elections were contended under different conditions than those found in precedent disputes. For the first time after the return to democracy, Lula would not be a candidate. The focus of the presidential election, which until then had been based on candidates grouping themselves as favorable or unfavorable to Lula, could not occur once again. But despite Lula not being a candidate, the trust of the people in him guided the elections, contended regarding the choice of voters who wanted his third term. The immediate effect of this strategy was that competitors converged to the political center and highlighted any of their characteristics that would make it possible to categorize them as 'political heirs of Lula.' As the electoral market is affected by previous rules, strategies took into account the mechanical and psychological effects of these norms and were adjusted to the demands of the voters. This resulted in the central axis of this election being less about *issues positions* and more about the dispute over the representation of the 'third term' of Lula.

The success of the "third term" strategy was made possible by the combination of the following conditions: (i) the presence of a reduced link between voters and parties, (ii) use of personalism in the appeals of the campaigns, (iii) weakened opposition, (iv) reduction of the number of competitors, which made the election a referendum, (v) psychological effect of rules in the useful vote, (v) public opinion satisfied with the administration of the President, and (vi) the possibility of transferring prestige from the president to the candidate for his succession.

The political communication during the Free Electoral Advertisement Time was fundamental to polarize the dispute by promoting the thesis of the plebiscitary election and consolidating the image of Dilma as a symbolic representative of Lula. As she was little known by the general public, the political marketing was crucial for Dilma to persuade the electorate. The president was able to transfer prestige to his successor and the victory of this strategy shows that the main explanatory key to the success of candidates in those elections has being the ability to place himself/herself as a messenger of the third term of Lula. More than a case study, the 2010 elections in Brazil show that short-term factors such as electoral campaigns matter in vote decisions. Furthermore, these results confirm the directional theory, stating that the current disputes are less articulated by the distribution of ideological parties on a one-dimensional scale and more by valences. Thus, further than being a reflection of demands in a perfect electoral market, candidates have been associated with valences, which emerge in elections as singular characteristics.

References

Baquero, M. and Linhares, B. F. (2011) 'Por que os brasileiros nãoconfiam nos partidos? Bases para compreender a cultura política (anti) partidária e possíveis saídas' in *Revista Debates,* 5(1): 89-114.

Beaudoux, V. G., D'Adamo, O. and Slavinsky, G. (2007) *Comunicación política y campañas electorales:* estrategias en elecciones presidenciales. Barcelona: Gedisa.

Bezerra, H. D. and Mundim, P. S. (2011) 'Qual foi o papel das variáveis midiáticas na eleição presidencial de 2010?' in *Opinião Pública*, 17: 452-476.

Camargo, Malco B. (1999) *Do Bolso para as Urnas: A Influência de Economia na Escolha entre Fernando Henrique e Lula nas Eleições de 1998*. Dissertação de Mestrado apresentada ao Instituto Universitário de Pesquisas do Rio de Janeiro.

Campbell, A., Converse, P. E., Miller, W. E. and Donald E. Stokes, D. E. (1960) *The American voter*. New York: Wiley.

Carreirão, Y.(2002) *A decisão de voto nas eleições presidenciais brasileira*,Rio de Janeiro/ Florianópolis: Editora da FGV/EDUFSC.

_____(2007) 'Identificação ideológica, partidos e voto na eleição presidencial de 2006' in *Opinião Pública*, 13(2): 307-339.

Coma, F. M. I.(2008) *¿Por qué importan las campañas electorales?*. Madrid: CIS – Centro de Investigaciones Sociológicas.

Converse, P. (1964) 'The nature of belief systems in mass publics' in D. E. Apter (ed.) *Ideology and discontent*. New York: Free Press.

Costa, O. and Marques, H. (2009) 'É muito difícil Lula transferir afeto' (Entrevista com Antônio Lavareda),*Isto É*, São Paulo, Edição 2079, s./p., 16 set 2009.. <http://www.istoe.com.br/ assuntos/entrevista/detalhe/18177_E+MUITO+DIF ICIL+LULA+TRANSFERIR+AFETO>. Accessed 27 February 2012.

Figueiredo, M. and Aldé, A. (2010) 'Intenção de voto e propaganda política: efeitos e gramáticas da propaganda eleitoral' in L. F. Miguel and F. Biroli (eds.) *Mídia, representação e democracia*. Hucitec.

Figueiredo, Marcus et. al, (2000) 'Estratégias de persuasão em eleições majoritárias: uma proposta metodológica para o estudo da propaganda eleitoral' in Figueiredo, Rubens et. al. (Org) *Marketing Político e Persuasão Eleitoral*. São Paulo: Fundação Konrad-Adenauer.

Fiorina, M, (1981) *Retrospective voting in American national elections*. New Haven: Yale University Press.

Holbrook, Thomas M. (1996) *Do campaigns matter?* London: Sage.

Key Jr., V. O. (1966) *The Responsible Electorate:* Rationality in Presidential Voting 1936-1960. Cambridge: Harvard University Press.

Lavareda, A., Telles, H de S. (2011) *Como o eleitor escolhe seu prefeito:* campanha e voto nas eleições municipais. Rio de Janeiro: Editora da Fundação Getúlio Vargas.

Lazarsfeld, P., Berelson, B. and Gaudet, H. (1948) *The people's choice*. New York: Columbia University Press.

Lewis-Bechk, M. et al. (2008) *The American Voter Revisited*. Ann Arbor: The University Michigan of Press.

Lourenço, L. (2007) *Abrindo a Caixa-Preta:* da indecisão à escolha. A eleição presidencial de 2002. Rio de janeiro. Tese (Doutorado em Ciências Políticas e Sociologia) – Instituto Universitário de Pesquisas do Rio de Janeiro (IUPERJ).

Lourenço, L. (2003) 'Ativação, reforço e cristalização: pistas sobre os efeitos o horário gratuito de propaganda eleitoral' in H. S. Telles and J. I Lucas. (Org.) *Das Ruas às Urnas:* partidos e eleições no Brasil contemporâneo. Caxias do Sul: EDUCS.

Manin, B. (1995) 'As metamorfoses do governo representative' in *RBCS,* ano 10, n. 29, p 5-34. Disponível em: http://www.anpocs.org.br/portal/publicacoes/rbcs_00_29/rbcs29_01. htm. Accessed 7 June.

Martinez, I. C. (Org) (2004) *Las campañas electorales y sus efectos en la decisión de voto.* Valencia: Tirant Lo Blanch.

Moisés, J. A. (Org) (2010) *Democracia e Confiança. Por que os cidadãos desconfiam das instituições públicas?* São Paulo: Edusp.

Montero, M. (1999) 'El análisis del discurso político o el fin de la inocencia" in Botello, G. Mota (Org.) *Psicología política del nuevo siglo.* México, D.F.: Somepso-Sep

Mundim, P. (2010) 'Cientistas Políticos, Comunicólogos e o Papel da Mídia nas Teorias da Decisão do Voto' in *Politica Hoje* v. 19.

Norris, P. (2009) *Derecha Radical: votantes y partidos políticos em el mercado electoral.* Madrid: AKAI.

Panke et al. (2011) 'O que os candidatos a Presidência do Brasil falaram nos programas do HGPE e nas últimas eleições'. *IV Encontro da Compolítica,* Universidade do Estado do Rio de Janeiro, 13 a 15 de abril de 2011. http://www.compolitica. org/home/wp-content/uploads/2011/03/Luciana-Panke.pdf Accessed 3 March 2011.

Rennó, L. and Cabello, A. (2010) 'As bases do lulismo: a volta do personalismo, realinhamento ideológico ou não alinhamento?' in *RBCS,* v. 25, n. 74

Rocha Neto, F. M. (2008) *La profesionalización de las campañas electorales en Brasil* (1989-2006). Universidad de Salamanca, Tese de Doutorado

Santos, R. D. dos (2009) *A economia política das eleições 2002.* Um estudo sobre a concentração de financiamento de campanha para Deputado Federal. Dissertação apresentada ao Departamento de Ciência Política do PPGCP (Programa de Pós-Graduação em Ciência Política do Instituto de Ciências Humanas e Filosofia) da Universidade Federal Fluminense. Niterói.

Silva, R. H. et al. (2011) 'A eleição de 2010 observada a partir da web: os usos (e abusos?) de novos veículos de participação pública'. *IV Congresso Latino Americano de Opinião Pública da Wapor.* Belo Horizonte

Speck, B. (2010a) 'O dinheiro e a política no Brasil' in *Le Monde Diplomatique.* São Paulo, n. 34. http://www.diplomatique.org.br/artigo.php?id=674&PHPSESSID =099cbc670a7e8a6c998a4f532aaf76c9. Accessed 2 March 2011.

_____, 2010 (b) 'Três idéias para oxigenar o debate sobre dinheiro e política no Brasil° in *Em Debate,* n. 12. Belo Horizonte. http://www.opiniaopublica. ufmg.br/emdebate/speck7. pdf. Accessed 27 February 2012.

Singer, A. (2009) 'Raízes Sociais e ideológicas do Lulismo' in *Novos Estudos CEBRAP,* São Paulo, n. 85.

_____ (2000) *Esquerda e direita no eleitorado brasileiro.* São Paulo: Edusp.

Soares, G. and Terron, S. L. (2008) 'Dois Lulas: a geografia eleitoral da reeleição (explorando conceitos, métodos e técnicas de análise geoespacial)' in *Opinião Pública,* Campinas, vol.14,2: 269- 301.

Stokes, D. E. (1963) 'Spatial Models of Party Competition' in *American Political Science Review,* 57: 368 - 77

Telles, H. de S. (2010) 'Uma eleição de manutenção do status quo' in *Le Monde Diplomatique.* São Paulo, n. 36. http://www.diplomatique.org.br/artigo. php?id=718. Accessed 28 February 2012.

Telles, H. de S. and Storni, T. P. (2011) 'Ideologias, atitudes e decisão de voto em eleitores de direita e esquerda' in *Revista Latinoamericana de Opinión Pública: investigación social aplicada,* 1: 87-148.

Telles, H. de S. and Dias, M. (2011) 'Condutas políticas, valores e voto dos eleitores jovens' in *Revista do Legislativo*, n. 43: 83-103. http://www.almg.gov.br/opencms/export/sites/default/consulte/publicacoes_assembleia/ periodicas/revistas/arquivos/pdfs/43/05_condutas_politicas_valores_voto_dos_eleitores_ jovens_bh.pdf Accessed 20 February 2012.

Telles, H. de S. and Ruiz, L. (2011) 'Elecciones Presidenciales brasileñas 2010: campaña electoral, presidente saliente y adscripción partidista' in *Congreso de la Asociación Española de Ciencia Política* (AECPA).

Terron, S. and Soares, G. (2010) 'As bases eleitorais de Lula e do PT: do distanciamento ao divórcio' in *Opinião Pública*, vol.16, 2: 310-337.

Veiga, L. (2001) *A busca de razões para o voto:* o uso que o eleitor faz do Horário Eleitoral. Tese (doutorado), Rio de Janeiro: Iuperj.

Zucco, C. (2008) 'The President's "New" Constituency: Lula and the Pragmatic Vote in Brazil's 2006 Presidential Elections' in *Journal of Latin American Studies*, 40: 29-49.

www.ingramcontent.com/pod-product-compliance
Lightning Source LLC
Chambersburg PA
CBHW072159270326
41930CB00011B/2482